Homage (and Criticism) to the Mediterranean City

Regional Sustainability and Economic Resilience

RIVER PUBLISHERS SERIES IN SOCIAL, URBAN, ECONOMIC AND ENVIRONMENTAL SUSTAINABILITY

The River Series on Social, Urban, Economic and Environmental Sustainability is a series of comprehensive academic and professional books which focus on the societal side of sustainability. The series focuses on topics ranging from theory to policy and real-life case studies and applications.

Books published in the series include research monographs, edited volumes, handbooks and textbooks. The books provide professionals, researchers, educators, and advanced students in the field with an invaluable insight into the latest research and developments.

Topics included in this series are as follows:-

- Climate Change Mitigation
- Renewable Energy Policy
- Urban sustainability
- Strategic environmental planning
- Environmental Systems Monitoring and Analysis
- Greening the World Economy
- Sustainable Development

For a list of other books in this series, visit www.riverpublishers.com

Homage (and Criticism) to the Mediterranean City

Regional Sustainability and Economic Resilience

Ioannis Vardopoulos
Harokopio University of Athens, Greece

Francisco Escrivà Saneugenio
University of Valencia, Spain

Adele Sateriano
Independent researcher, Rome, Italy

Luca Salvati
Sapienza University of Rome, Italy

River Publishers

Routledge
Taylor & Francis Group
NEW YORK AND LONDON

Published 2024 by River Publishers
River Publishers
Alsbjergvej 10, 9260 Gistrup, Denmark
www.riverpublishers.com

Distributed exclusively by Routledge
605 Third Avenue, New York, NY 10017, USA
4 Park Square, Milton Park, Abingdon, Oxon OX14 4RN

Homage (and Criticism) to the Mediterranean City: Regional Sustainability and Economic Resilience / Ioannis Vardopoulos, Francisco Escrivà Saneugenio, Adele Sateriano and Luca Salvati.

Routledge is an imprint of the Taylor & Francis Group, an informa business

ISBN 978-87-7004-177-5 (hardback)
ISBN 978-87-7004-191-1 (paperback)
ISBN 978-10-4012-603-5 (online)
ISBN 978-1-003-51730-6 (ebook master)

Contents

Foreword

In the colorful tapestry of urban landscapes, the Mediterranean city stands as a testament to resilience, sustainability, and the enduring spirit of human civilization.

Within this volume, navigating the interweaving pathways of Mediterranean urbanity, with its intricate streets, and bustling squares, readers are confronted with the challenges of preserving the past while embracing the future, and the delicate balance between urbanization and sustainability.

The chapters, through meticulous scholarly analyses, offer a rich spectrum of perspectives, from the socio-ecological dynamics of soil sealing to the nuances of settlement patterns and socio-environmental interactions. The authors challenge conventional notions of sprawl and development, instigating a more holistic approach that respects the unique Mediterranean contextual character and heritage.

Whether you find yourself crafting policy, designing the cities of tomorrow, advocating for change as a concerned citizen, or simply as a student eager to learn and contribute in this field, this book provides invaluable insights and inspiration for all.

According with the book's thinking, there is no 'one-fits-all' policy positively contributing to the long-term development of Mediterranean cities. Instead, sustainable and resilient solutions to the negative externalities of urban growth come from a balanced mix of formal and informal actions. These should be calibrated and finetuned at the appropriate scale, exploiting opportunities and managing challenges inherent in the peculiarities of the regional dynamics, while addressing the diverse responses of local governance and communities to external stimuli.

Andreas Savvides
Architect and City Planner
Associate Professor, University of Cyprus
f. Chair, Department of Architecture, University of Cyprus
Vice-Chair, Planning Board, Republic of Cyprus

List of Figures

List of Tables

1

Mediterranean Cities, Regional Sustainability, and Economic Resilience

Ioannis Vardopoulos, Francisco Escrivà Saneugenio, Adele Sateriano, and Luca Salvati

The current work endeavors to establish an interpretative framework, employing both narrative and quantitative analyses, to elucidate the short-term dynamics within burgeoning Mediterranean cities, building upon the seminal work "The Mediterranean city in transition" by Lila Leontidou, which was published three decades ago (Leontidou, 1990). This framework, while specifically tailored to the unique morphological and functional characteristics of Mediterranean cities, is designed to be adaptable and applicable to urban areas, metropolitan regions, and cities worldwide that share similar attributes.

Departing from conventional narratives centered on economic stagnation and social secularism (Nickayin *et al.*, 2021), this study offers a fresh perspective on Mediterranean urbanities, positing their correlation with housing and welfare regimes (Zambon and Salvati, 2019), societal transformations (Egidi *et al.*, 2023), local governance structures (Vinci and Salvati, 2022), and deficiencies in spatial planning (Doukas *et al.*, 2022; Vardopoulos *et al.*, 2023). The analysis delves into the neglected potential for mitigating regional disparities (*e.g.* Salvia *et al.*, 2022), conducting a meticulous examination of environmental disparities (Salvati *et al.*, 2017), economic imbalances (Petrakos *et al.*, 2023), and overarching social inequalities (Benassi *et al.*, 2023). The outcome aims to furnish an integrated, and potentially holistic, understanding of spatial divisions between cities and their surrounding territories.

The interpretation derives benefit from a comparative investigation of ecologically fragile and socially unstable Mediterranean contexts (Tombolini *et al.*, 2023), with value ascribed to the scenic and cultural attributes of cities and the surrounding countryside (Manola, 2022; Stavroudakis *et al.*, 2013). In the face of a persistent crisis impacting economic systems, institutions, and local governance structures (Garefalakis *et al.*, 2017; Maris *et al.*, 2022; Salvati, 2018), a new dynamic path characteristic of regional development in Southern Europe is observed, wherein social classes play a pivotal role (Di Feliciantonio and Salvati, 2014). A broader discussion on the future development of Mediterranean cities is stimulated, emphasizing the inherent short-term divergence in urban and rural regions and a common trend toward economic convergence over a longer time window.

The pursuit of a unified definition for the "Mediterranean city" stereotype has led to the imposition of forced taxonomies reflecting artifact views of several Southern European regions (Carlucci, 2017). Positioned as a hegemonic notion straddling geography, economics, and sociology, a novel interpretation of the "Mediterranean city" stereotype is presented in this work through the examination of key operational dimensions. Attention is specifically directed toward processes such as "urban sprawl" (Zambon *et al.*, 2017), "land-use changes" (Vardopoulos, 2023), "social conflict" (Perrin *et al.*, 2018), and "economic polarizations" (D'Agata *et al.*, 2023), thereby elucidating critical socioeconomic issues and departing from the "metaphorical vision" that has historically characterized the discourse on Mediterranean urbanities (Leontidou, 1990).

Despite being regarded as some of the most compact cities in Europe (Vardopoulos *et al.*, 2023; Salvati, 2016), Mediterranean cities have experienced a shift from compact-dense structures (Figure 1.1) to more "dispersed" and discontinuous morphologies that extend into surrounding lands (Schneider and Woodcock, 2008; Zitti *et al.*, 2018). Residential settlements, transforming dispersed (rural) villages, and isolated buildings, along with commercial units, industrial headquarters, and tourism resorts increasingly linked by a pervasive road network (Vardopoulos *et al.*, 2023; Trikalitis and Manola, 2023), have become the prevalent characteristics of the "sprawled" Mediterranean city (Chorianopoulos *et al.*, 2010; Salvia *et al.*, 2018).

Due to the "compactness-sprawl tension" prevalent in contemporary Mediterranean cities, land-use stratification is posited as a consequence of socioeconomic dynamics involving multiple agents (Salvati, 2016). Mediterranean suburbs, as defined by Salvati and Zitti (2007), are regarded as laboratories of land-use change, where a stratification of immediate factors and underlying causes fosters an unequal, unbalanced, and unsustainable conversion of pervious land to urban use (Soliman *et al.*, 2004; Salvati and Zitti, 2007; Jomaa *et al.*, 2008; Marull *et al.*, 2009). Territorial constraints and local dynamics have contributed to the inherent stratification of socioeconomic forces that shape landscape forms and territorial functions in the Mediterranean region (Briassoulis, 2001; Garcia Latorre *et al.*, 2001; Antrop,

Figure 1.1 The kaleidoscopic Mediterranean city: the stratification of styles, forms, and communities in Arc de Triomf, downtown Barcelona. Source: Authors' photographic archive.

2004; Polyzos *et al.*, 2008; Geri *et al.*, 2010). Changes in factors such as population, resources, technology, and institutions have led to spatially balanced land-use transitions, reflecting complex socio-demographic features across the administrative boundaries of both central cities and suburbs (Tanrivermis, 2003; Kasanko *et al.*, 2006; Longhi and Musolesi, 2007; Marull *et al.*, 2009). The governance of land-use through innovative planning solutions may benefit from diachronic and comparative analyses of landscape change in cities with varied morphology, population structure, and landscape dynamics (Xu *et al.*, 2018; Kempton *et al.*, 2022).

Navigating 'Urban Tapestries': Exploring Sustainability, Resilience, and Sprawl in Contemporary Mediterranean Cities

Athens serves as a representative example in this study, illustrating the transformation from a compact and dense mono-centric city to one characterized by "sprawled development" over recent decades. The study area encompasses a substantial portion of the NUTS-2 region of Attica, delineated by the boundaries of the metropolitan region considered in the Urban

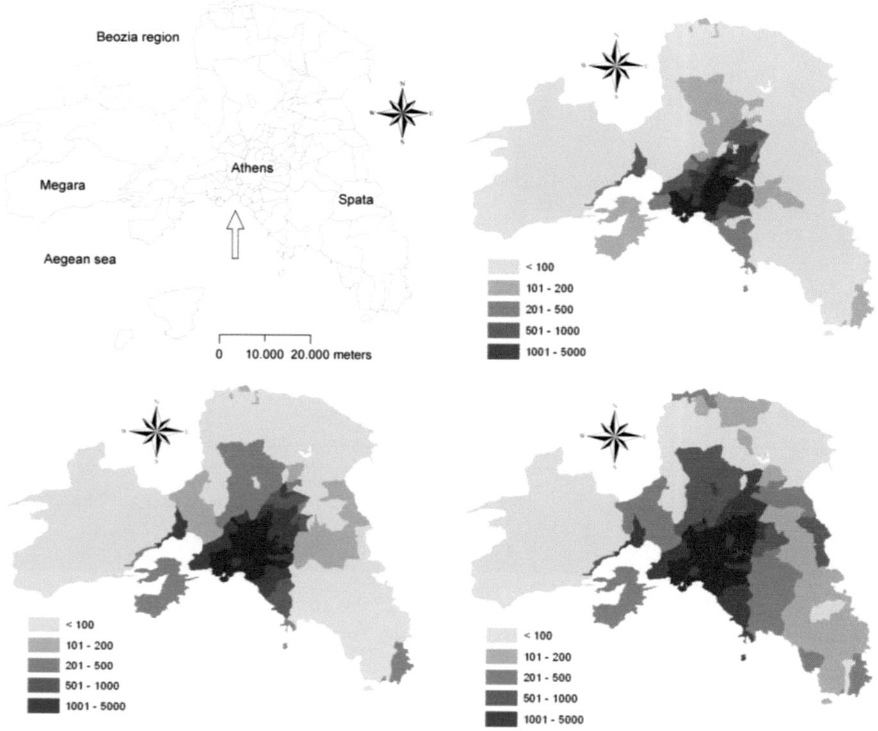

Figure 1.2 Map of the study area in Greece with municipal boundaries (left); population density (inhabitants/km^2) in metropolitan Athens, selected years (upper right: 1951; lower left: 1991; lower right: 2021). Source: Authors' own elaboration on Hellenic Statistical Authority (ELSTAT).

Atlas project (European Environment Agency, 2010; Ciommi *et al.*, 2022). This area is further divided into 115 municipalities, with 58 constituting the strictly urban conurbation covering 430 km^2. The entire land area of mainland municipalities (Greek: δήμοι, romanized: *dímoi*) and municipal communities (Greek: δημοτικές κοινότητες, romanized: *dimotikés koinótites*) within the administrative region of Attica, including Salamina (Greek: Σαλαμίνα, romanized: *Salamína*) Island, encompasses 3,025 km^2 (Figure 1.2). The city region is predominantly characterized by mountains bordering the urban area of Athens, with three coastal plains – Messoghia plain, Marathon plain, and Thriasio plain – situated in the Attica region outside greater Athens (Salvati *et al.*, 2010).

Athens has undergone one of the most rapid population growths in continental Europe (Table 1.1), displaying expansion rates comparable to

Table 1.1 Population and settlement expansion in metropolitan Athens, 1961–2021.

Year	Population density*	Annual population growth, %	Suburban population, %	Inhabitants per building**
1961	669	2.5	8.4	14.9
1991	1154	0.4	12.4	5.7
2021	1340	0.1	15.9	4.9

(*) Inhabitants per km^2; (**) includes residential and service buildings.
Source: Authors' own elaboration on data released by Hellenic Statistical Authority (ELSTAT).

those observed in developing countries (Nikolakopoulos *et al.*, 2005). By the 1950s, the city had fully developed all available open spaces, sealing off free land (Tsilika and Vardopoulos, 2022). Over a mere decade (1951–1961), the population surged by nearly 250,000 inhabitants, surpassing 850 thousand inhabitants by 1971 (Vinci *et al.*, 2022). Following a gradual decline in the industrial sector (see Vardopoulos *et al.*, 2021), the consolidation of peripheral areas became more pronounced in the western part of the capital during 1971–1981, though heightened activity was observed in both the northern and eastern regions (Salvia *et al.*, 2020).

The proportion of the population residing in the urban area peaked at 92% of the population in Attica in 1961, gradually decreasing to approximately 80% in 2011. Consequently, the urban area relinquished its monocentric characteristic, assuming a new morphology that spread more evenly across lowland Attica (Salvati, 2015). A discernible trend toward discontinuous expansion only became evident in the 1980s (Vinci *et al.*, 2023).

Between the early-1990s and the early-2020s, Athens underwent a predominantly dispersed expansion, spurred by the 2004 Olympics (see Mitoula *et al.*, 2008; Theodoropoulou *et al.*, 2009) and extending across the entirety of Attica, notably Mesogeia – a rural region situated 30 km east of the capital, identified as the focal point of Athenian sprawl (Couch *et al.*, 2007; Karaveli and Doukas, 2012). The morphology of Athens manifested a combination of "compact growth" and more recent "discontinuous expansion" waves (Figure 1.3), resulting in distinct urban areas characterized by density and dispersion, respectively (Salvati, 2014; Doukas, 2011). In 1960, urban fabric covered 12% of the surveyed area, expanding to 27% by 2018. The evolution of land-use in Athens reflects laissez-faire urbanism (see Zambon *et al.*, 2017), deregulated planning, and informal processes of city expansion, phenomena frequently observed in other Mediterranean contexts (Weber and Puissant, 2003; Richardson and Chang-Lee, 2004; Paul and Tonts, 2005; Turok and Mykhnenko, 2007).

Figure 1.3 Urban kaleidoscopes: Athens' dance between compactness. Source: Own adaptation of public photographic sources.

Unraveling the Labyrinth: A Scholarly Expedition into the Dynamics of the Mediterranean Urban Sprawl

The "Mediterranean city" paradigm has made a positive contribution to urban geography by challenging reductionist and mechanistic approaches to the exploration of form–function relationships (Salvati *et al.*, 2015), as extensively discussed in Chapter 2. Despite the evident shift of certain Mediterranean cities toward "western" and "northern" urban models deeply integrated into the global economy, this interpretation retains a degree of relevance and significance within a transitional context following a prolonged crisis (Carlucci *et al.*, 2017). While population growth continues to serve as the "engine" of Mediterranean urbanization, it has also thrust Southern European metropolises into the forefront of new critical challenges, such as the socio-environmental ramifications of a substantial rural exodus (Maravegias and Doukas. 20121; Egidi *et al.*, 2020). The abrupt setbacks in certain development policies, aimed at economic modernization (Spindler and Forrester, 1993), local competitiveness (Enright, 2000), and urban regeneration (Vardopoulos *et al.*, 2020), have played a pivotal role in shaping characteristic patterns and socioeconomic processes of metropolitan growth in this region (Carlucci *et al.*, 2023).

From this perspective, urban sprawl, land-use change, social dynamics, and the ensuing processes of economic polarization in a rapidly evolving Mediterranean region are scrutinized. This involves a critical examination of both traditional theories of urban growth and the structural models emblematic of a singular "Mediterranean city" stereotype. Comparative and diachronic approaches are adopted, considering them as substantial contributors to the discourse on sprawling Mediterranean cities and their socioeconomic interplay with the surrounding environments (Kourlourios, 1997; Dura-Guimera, 2003; Muñoz, 2003; Marull *et al.*, 2009; D'Agata *et al.*, 2024).

In Chapter 3, an extrinsic representation of sprawl was established by examining the spatial pattern of land imperviousness in metropolitan Athens (see D'Agata *et al.*, 2023). The analysis highlights the significance of simple (small-scale) indicators that elucidate soil sealing processes driven by urbanization, offering insights for urban containment policies and spatial planning aiming at zero-net land consumption. Three municipal typologies (strictly urban, intermediate, and strictly rural) were discerned, each displaying distinct soil sealing profiles. The spatial distribution of land imperviousness unmistakably mirrors the shift from mono-centric and compact forms to polycentric and more dispersed agglomerations (D'Agata *et al.*, 2024).

As delineated in earlier chapters, cities within advanced economies underwent expansion under diverse economic conditions, resulting in a myriad of development trajectories (Salvati *et al.*, 2015). The spatial heterogeneity observed in contemporary urbanization justifies the application of quantitative approaches to identify novel relationships between form and function (Li *et al.*, 2019). Transitioning toward a land-use perspective that centers on settlement structure, Chapter 4 introduces a quantitative approach that measures settlement compactness (or dispersion) based on the density of detached buildings in the total stock. The expansion of settlements is suggested to hinge on the intricate interplay of socioeconomic factors, territorial limitations, and regulatory frameworks (Kuznetsova, 2019).

By reconnecting a structural analysis of heterogeneous urban fabrics with a functional profile of metropolitan areas, the empirical findings delineate the role of spatial planning in finely regulating dispersed urbanization (Vasta, 2019). The pursuit of a finely tuned policy for zero-net land consumption necessitates a sustainable and spatially balanced urbanization, particularly in contexts where informal settlements have been the driving force behind urban growth for decades (Marquard *et al.*, 2020). Strategies for sustainable development oriented toward settlement containment should forge more effective interfaces with local contexts, leveraging the benefits of place-based actions (Vardopoulos, 2022). Studies examining the relationship between the form and functions of cities unquestionably highlight sprawl as a captivating subject, unveiling inherent differences on a local scale (Rojas *et al.*, 2013; Glaeser and Kahn, 2004). In this context, Mediterranean cities present a comprehensive panorama of sprawl types that may necessitate specific assessment tools (Salvati and Morelli, 2014). In order to offer an innovative quantification of recent urbanization processes in the Mediterranean, Chapter 5 introduces residential swimming pools as a "sprawl landmark." Derived from this element, the proposed indicators are designed to meet fundamental criteria, including easy computation and graphical representation, flexibility, affordability, and comprehensibility to non-technical stakeholders.

In this context, new spatial relationships have emerged among cities, territories, and landscapes, gradually overshadowing the role of urban–rural gradients in the last half-century. Confronting complex realities and the increasingly debated regional issues, regional analysis has garnered significant interest in recent years. An analysis of the spontaneous development of diversified economic activities, exerting an increased impact on fragile environments, provides the foundational knowledge for discussing suitable practices and projects aimed at the sustainable recovery of degraded areas. The industrialization of the area and the associated land-use changes unfolded through a sequence of official revisions of zoning plans confirms how sprawl and the preservation of rural landscapes on the fringe are interconnected issues in advanced economies (Patacchini and Zenou, 2009).

A comprehensive analysis of the relationship between rural landscapes and the expanding Mediterranean city definitely allows exploring potential implications for the sustainable management of suburban land. The integration of eco-sustainable planning with multifaceted research and policy dimensions (*e.g.*, social, economic, cultural, and political issues) characterizing Mediterranean regions represents a pertinent approach to urban fringe sustainability (Feleki *et al.*, 2018; Kempton, 2022; Vardopoulos *et al.*, 2023; Ragazou *et al.*, 2022a). The continuous assessment of these factors allows for the implementation of diverse development scenarios (Figure 1.4).

Collectively, the cases examined in this book illustrate how sprawl is unequivocally transforming Mediterranean fringes into "hybrid" landscapes. Land consumption yields significant environmental implications as it impacts land quality and initiates soil degradation (Garcia Latorre *et al.*, 2001; Losco and de Biase, 2021). Both ecological dynamics and socioeconomic processes were demonstrated to be catalysts for land consumption, consistent with the wider literature (Lambin and Meyfroidt, 2010; Ragazou *et al.*, 2022b). Informal settlements, spontaneous activities, house speculation, "laissez-faire" policies, and planning deregulation (Figure 1.5) emerged as pivotal drivers of spatial inequalities in land-use and its changes over time

Figure 1.4 Second-home settlements and tourism resorts at the base of the increased human pressure along the Mediterranean Sea coast, Cullera (Valencia), Spain. Source: Authors' photographic archive.

(Seto and Kaufmann, 2003; Ding, 2004; Rodríguez-Pose and Storper, 2020). These factors played a leading – albeit indirect – role in the economic marginalization of farmers, habitat fragmentation, and widespread land abandonment (Alphan, 2003; Tanrivermis, 2003; Aguilar, 2008).

Toward Sustainable Pathways? Crafting a "Mediterranean" Paradigm in Urban Planning

Despite the varying planning systems in Southern European countries (Giannakourou, 2005), policies aimed at curbing sprawl have demonstrated their weaknesses in most of the investigated contexts. Concurrently, the evolving relationship between land-use types is a potential outcome of a continuous process of "landscape homologation" (Salvati *et al.*, 2013). These transformations delineate a kind of "anthropogenic" landscape, awaiting land speculation and future urbanization (Christopoulou *et al.*, 2007). Taken together, the findings of the current work hold particular significance in developing "soft"

Figure 1.5 "Unsustainable" compactness and uneven growth of settlements planned in Southern Athens illustrated in a map sketch taken from the city master plan in the mid-1970s. Source: Own adaptation from the archives of the Hellenic Ministry of Environment.

theoretical models that explore land-use changes and in fostering a debate on potential tools for monitoring urban expansion. They may also contribute to designing policies that promote sustainable urban growth, the containment of soil sealing, and the conservation of high-quality land (Marull and Mallarach, 2005; Terzi and Bolen, 2009; Munafò *et al.*, 2011).

Drawing from these foundations, the promotion of monitoring approaches rooted in both narrative and quantitative analysis is strongly advocated. On one hand, the significance of statistical data and indicators is paramount in comprehending the primary functional and morphological attributes of Mediterranean urban regions undergoing rapid evolution toward metropolitan models centered on high-return services, infrastructure, and land speculation. On the other hand, the search for narratives, metaphors, and horizons to describe the evolution of urban fringes persists, as statistics and models often prove inadequate in capturing and interpreting the effects of latent socioeconomic factors that characterize both urban and suburban dynamics in the Mediterranean region.

Regional planning ought to champion multi-scale measures aimed at safeguarding sensitive landscape elements as hotspots for containing urban spillover. These measures should be integral components of a sustainable development strategy with the ultimate goal of alleviating territorial disparities. Failing to do so could entail the risk that rapid land-use changes in suburban areas may reshape residents' perceptions of environmental vulnerability and depletion of natural resources, while public officials adhere to a traditional sectoral and structural interpretation of land conservation as a strictly agricultural problem (Eakin *et al.*, 2009). Ultimately, the current planning system should more effectively consider the heightened role of urban sprawl as a driver for land vulnerability to degradation at the regional scale (Salvati and Zitti, 2007).

References

Aguilar, A. G. (2008). Peri-urbanization, illegal settlements and environmental impact in Mexico City. Cities, 25, 133–145.

Alphan, H. (2003). Land use change and urbanisation of Adana, Turkey. Land Degradation & Development, 14, 575–586.

Anas, A. (2013). Modelling in Urban and Regional Economics. Taylor & Francis, London.

Angel, S., Parent, J., Civco, D. L., Blei, A., and Potere, D. (2011). The dimensions of global urban expansion: Estimates and projections for all countries, 2000–2050. Progress in Planning, 75(2), 53–107.

Antrop, M., (2000). Changing patterns in the urbanized countryside of Western Europe. Landscape Ecology, 15, 257–270.

Ashby, J., Cox, D., and McInroy, N. (2009). An International Perspective of Local Government as Steward of Local Economic Resilience. Report by the Centre for Local Economic Strategies: Manchester.

Barata Salgueiro, T.B. (2001). Lisboa. Periferia e Centralidades. Oeiras: Celta.

Benassi, F., Naccarato, A., Iglesias-Pascual, R., Salvati, L., and Strozza, S. (2023). Measuring residential segregation in multi-ethnic and unequal European cities. International Migration, 61(2), 341–361.

Beriatos, E., and Gospodini, A. (2004). "Glocalising" urban landscapes: Athens and the 2004 Olympics. Cities, 21, 187–202.

Betteley, D. D., and Valler, D. (2000). Integrating the economic and the social: Policy and institutional change in local economic strategy. Local Economy, 14(4), 295–312.

Bianchini, L., Marucci, A., Sateriano, A., Di Stefano, V., Alemanno, R., and Colantoni, A. (2021). Urbanization and long-term forest dynamics in a metropolitan region of southern Europe (1936–2018). Sustainability, 13(21), 12164.

Biasi, R., Brunori, E., Smiraglia, D., and Salvati, L. (2015). Linking traditional tree-crop landscapes and agro-biodiversity in Central Italy using a database of typical and traditional products: A multiple risk assessment through a data mining analysis. Biodiversity and Conservation, 24, 3009–3031.

Briassoulis, H. (2001). Policy-oriented integrated analysis of land use change: An analysis of data needs. Environmental Management, 27, 1–11.

Bristow, G., and Wells, P. (2005). Innovative discourse for sustainable local development: A critical analysis of eco-industrialism. International Journal of Innovation and Sustainable Development, 1, 168–179.

Brouwer, F. B., Thomas, A. J., and Chadwick, M. J. (1991). Land use changes in Europe. Processes of change, environmental transformations and future patterns. Kluwer Academic Publishers, Dordrecht, 530 pp.

Brown, J., and Dillard, J. (2013). Agonizing over engagement: SEA and the "death of environmentalism" debates. Critical Perspectives on Accounting, 24(1), 1–18.

Bruegmann, R. (2005). Sprawl: a compact history. University of Chicago Press, Chicago, 301 pp.

Bryant, C.R., Russwurm, L.H., and McLellan, A.G. (1982). The city's countryside. Land and its management in the rural-urban fringe. Longman, London and New York, 249 pp.

Burgel, G. (2004). Athènes, de la balkanisation à la mondialisation. Méditerranée, 103(3-4), 59–63.

Busquets, J. 2006. Barcelona: the urban evolution of a compact city. Actar, Barcelona, 144 pp.

Cakir, G., Un, C., Baskent, E. Z., Kose, S., Sivrikaya, F., and Keles, S. (2008). Evaluating urbanization, fragmentation and land use/cover change pattern in Istambul city, Turkey from 1971 to 2002. Land Degradation & Development, 19, 663–675.

Carlucci, M., Chelli, F. M., and Salvati, L. (2018). Toward a new cycle: Short-term population dynamics, gentrification, and re-urbanization of Milan (Italy). Sustainability, 10(9), 3014.

Carlucci, M., Grigoriadis, E., Rontos, K., and Salvati, L. (2017). Revisiting a hegemonic concept: Long-term 'Mediterranean urbanization' in between city re-polarization and metropolitan decline. Applied Spatial Analysis and Policy, 10(3), 347–362.

Carlucci, M., Polinesi, G., and Salvati, L. (2023). Agglomeration v s amenities? Unraveling the latent engine of growth in metropolitan Greece. Environment and Planning B: Urban Analytics and City Science, 50(9), 2491–2509.

Carlucci, M., Zambon, I., and Salvati, L. (2019). Diversification in urban functions as a measure of metropolitan complexity. Environment and Planning B: Urban Analytics and City Science, 47(7), 1289–1305.

Cassiers, T., and Kesteloot, C. (2012). Socio-spatial inequalities and social cohesion in European cities. Urban Studies, 49(9), 1909–1924.

Catalàn, B., Sauri, D., and Serra, P. (2008). Urban sprawl in the Mediterranean? Patterns of growth and change in the Barcelona Metropolitan Region 1993–2000. Landscape and Urban Planning, 85(3–4), 174–184.

Cecchini, M., Zambon, I., Pontrandolfi, A., Turco, R., Colantoni, A., Mavrakis, A., and Salvati, L. (2019). Urban sprawl and the 'olive' landscape: Sustainable land management for 'crisis' cities. GeoJournal, 84(1), 237–255.

Chelli, F. M., Ciommi, M., Emili, A., Gigliarano, C., and Taralli, S. (2016). Assessing the Equitable and Sustainable Well-Being of the Italian Provinces. International Journal of Uncertainty, Fuzziness and Knowlege-Based Systems, 24, 39–62.

Chorianopoulos, I., Pagonis, T., Koukoulas, S., and Drymoniti, S. (2010). Planning, competitiveness and sprawl in the Mediterranean city: The case of Athens. Cities, 27, 249–259.

Christopoulou, O., Polyzos, S., and Minetos, D. (2007). Peri-urban and urban forests in Greece: Obstacle or advantage to urban development? Management of Environmental Quality, 18(4), 382–395.

Ciommi, M., Chelli, F. M., Carlucci, M., and Salvati, L. (2018). Urban growth and demographic dynamics in southern Europe: Toward a new statistical approach to regional science. Sustainability, 108(1), 2765.

Ciommi, M., Chelli, F. M., and Salvati, L. (2019). Integrating parametric and non-parametric multivariate analysis of urban growth and commuting patterns in a European metropolitan area. Quality and Quantity, 53(2), 957–979.

Ciommi, M., Egidi, G., Vardopoulos, I., Chelli, F. M., and Salvati, L. (2022). Toward a 'Migrant Trap'? Local Development, Urban Sustainability, Sociodemographic Inequalities, and the Economic Decline in a Mediterranean Metropolis. Social Sciences, 12(1), 26.

Ciommi, M., Gigliarano, C., Emili, A., Taralli, S., and Chelli, F. M. (2017). A new class of composite indicators for measuring well-being at the local level: An application to the Equitable and Sustainable Well-being (BES) of the Italian Provinces. Ecological Indicators, 76, 281–296.

Colantoni, A., Mavrakis, A., Sorgi, T., and Salvati, L. (2015). Towards a 'polycentric' landscape? Reconnecting fragments into an integrated network of coastal forests in Rome. Rendiconti Lincei 26(3), 615–624.

Costa, F., Noble, A. G., and Pendleton, G. (1991). Evolving planning systems in Madrid, Rome, and Athens. Geojournal, 24, 293–303.

Couch, C., Petschel-held, G., and Leontidou, L. (2007). Urban Sprawl in Europe: Landscapes, Land-use Change and Policy. London: Blackwell.

Cuadrado-Ciuraneta, S., Durà-Guimerà, A., and Salvati, L. (2017). Not only tourism: Unravelling suburbanization, second-home expansion and "rural" sprawl in Catalonia, Spain. Urban Geography, 38(1), 66–89.

D'Agata, A., Ponza, D., Stroiu, F. A., Vardopoulos, I., Rontos, K., Escrivà, F., Chelli, F., Alaimo, L. S., Salvati, L., and Nickyain, S. S. (2023). Toward sustainable development trajectories? Estimating urban footprints from high-resolution copernicus layers in Athens, Greece. Land, 12(8), 1490.

De Rosa, S., and Salvati, L. (2016). Beyond a 'side street story'? Naples from spontaneous centrality to entropic polycentricism, towards a 'crisis city.' Cities, 51, 74–83.

Delladetsima, P. M. (2006). The emerging property development pattern in Greece and its impact on spatial development. European Urban and Regional Studies, 13(3), 245–278.

Di Feliciantonio, C., and Salvati, L. (2015). 'Southern' Alternatives of Urban Diffusion: Investigating Settlement Characteristics and Socio-Economic Patterns in Three Mediterranean Regions. Tijdschrift Voor Economische En Sociale Geografie, 106(4), 453–470.

Di Feliciantonio, C., Salvati, L., Sarantakou, E., and Rontos, K. (2018). Class diversification, economic growth and urban sprawl: Evidence from a pre-crisis European city. Quality and Quantity, 52(4), 1501–1522.

Ding, C. (2004). Urban Spatial Development in the Land Policy Reform Era: Evidence from Beijing. Urban Studies, 41(10), 1889–1907.

Domènech, E., and Saurí, D. (2006). Urbanization and water consumption: Influencing factors in the metropolitan region of Barcelona. Urban Studies, 43(9), 1605–1623.

Doukas, Y. E. (2011). Economic activity and productivity: The role of density in the Greek urban space. European Association of Geographers Annual Meeting "Geography: Your World – A European Perspective", 2-5 June 2011. Athens, Greece.

Doukas, Y. E., Maravegias, N., and Andreou, G. (Eds.). (2022). Η χωρική διάσταση της ευρωπαϊκής ολοκλήρωσης: σύγκλιση ή απόκλιση; Dionicos: Athens, Greece. ISBN: 978-6185-6650-3-6.

Dura-Guimera, A. (2003). Population deconcentration and social restructuring in Barcelona, a European Mediterranean city. Cities, 20, 387–394.

Eakin, H., Lerner, A. M., and Murtinho, F. (2010). Adaptive capacity in evolving peri-urban spaces: responses to flood risk in the Upper Lerma River Valley, Mexico. Global Environmental Change, 20(1), 14–22.

Economidou, E. (1993). The Attic landscape throughout the centuries and its human degradation. Landscape and Urban Planning, 24, 33–37.

Egidi, G., Halbac-Cotoara-Zamfir, R., Cividino, S., Quaranta, G., Salvati, L., and Colantoni, A. (2020). Rural in Town: Traditional Agriculture, Population Trends, and Long-Term Urban Expansion in Metropolitan Rome. Land, 9(2), 53.

Egidi, G., Mosconi, E. M., Turco, R., and Salvati, L. (2023). Functions follow structures? The long-term evolution of economic dynamics, social transformations, and landscape morphology in a Mediterranean metropolis. Land Use Policy, 129, 106659.

Enright, M. J. (2000). The Globalization of Competition and the Localization of Competitive Advantage: Policies towards Regional Clustering. In The Globalization of Multinational Enterprise Activity and Economic Development (pp. 303–331). Palgrave Macmillan UK.

European Environment Agency (2006). Urban sprawl in Europe – The ignored challenge. Copenhagen: EEA Report No. 10.

Feleki, E., Achillas, C., Vlachokostas, C., Michailidou, A., Ortega, L., and Moussiopoulos, N. (2018). Preservation of the Mediterranean Identity: An Intra-City Analysis Towards a Macro-Regional Approach for the Characterisation of Urban Sustainability. Sustainability, 10(10), 3551.

Ferrara, A., Kelly, C., Wilson, G. A., Nolè, A., Mancino, G., Bajocco, S., and Salvati, L. (2016). Shaping the role of'fast'and'slow'drivers of change in forest-shrubland socio-ecological systems. Journal of Environmental Management, 169, 155–166.

Ferrara, C., Carlucci, M., Grigoriadis, E., Corona, P., and Salvati, L. (2017). A comprehensive insight into the geography of forest cover in Italy: Exploring the importance of socioeconomic local contexts. Forest Policy and Economics, 75, 12–22.

Florida, R. (2011). The Great Reset: How New Ways of Living and Working Drive Postcrash Prosperity. Florida: Random House Canada.

Frenkel, A., and Ashkenazi, M. (2008). Measuring urban sprawl: How can we deal with it? Environment and Planning B: Planning and Design, 35(1), 56–79.

Gaffikin, F., and Perry, D. C. (2012). The contemporary urban condition: Understanding the globalizing city as informal, contested, and anchored. Urban Affairs Review, 48(5), 701–730.

Garcia Latorre, J., Garcia-Latorre, J., and Sanchez-Picon, A. (2001). Dealing with aridity: socio-economic structures and environmental changes in an arid Mediterranean region. Land Use Policy, 18, 53–64.

Garcia-López, M. A., and Muniz, I. (2010). Employment decentralisation: Poly-centricity or scatteration? The case of Barcelona. Urban Studies, 47(14), 3035–3056.

Genske, D.D. (2003). Urban Land – Degradation, Investigation, Remediation. Springer, Berlin. Heidelberg, New York, 333 pp.

Giannakourou, G. (2005). Transforming spatial planning policy in Mediterranean countries: Europeanization and domestic change. European Planning Studies, 13, 319–331.

Gibbs, D. (1997). Urban sustainability and economic development in the United Kingdom: Exploring the contradictions. Cities, 14(4), 203–208.

Gigliarano, C., and Chelli, F. M. (2016). Measuring inter-temporal intragenerational mobility: an application to the Italian labour market. Quality and Quantity, 50(1), 89–102.

Glaeser, E. L., and Kahn, M. E. (2004). Sprawl and urban growth. In Handbook of Regional and Urban Economics, (pp. 2481–2527). Elsevier.

Glaster, G., Hanson, R., Ratcliffe, M. R., Wolman, H., Coleman, S., and Freihage, J. (2001). Wrestling sprawl to the ground: Defining and measuring an elusive concept. Housing Policy Debate, 12(4), 681–717.

Gonzales, S. (2011). The north/south divide in Italy and England: Discursive construction of regional inequality. European Urban and Regional Studies, 18(1), 62–76.

Gordon, P., and Richardson, H. W. (2000). Are compact cities a desirable planning goal? Journal of the American Planning Association, 63(1), 89–106.

Gospodini, A. (2009). Post-industrial trajectories of Mediterranean European cities: the case of post-Olympics Athens. Urban Studies, 46(5/6), 1157–1186.

Halbac-Cotoara-Zamfir, R., Marucci, A., Salvia, R., Quaranta, G., Sateriano, A., Cecchini, M., and Bianchini, L. (2022). Caring of the Fringe? Mediterranean Desertification between Peri-Urban Ecology and Socioeconomics. Sustainability, 14(3), 1426.

Hall, P., and Pain, K. (2006). The Polycentric Metropolis. Learning from Mega-city Regions in Europe. London, Earthscan.

Karaveli, E., and Doukas, Y. E. (2012). Rural development policy: An alternative development strategy for the case of Greece. Region & Periphery, 2, 21.

Kazepov, Y. (2005). Cities of Europe: Changing Contexts, Local Arrangements, and the Challenge to Urban Cohesion. Oxford, Blackwell.

Kempton, Y., Salvati, L., and Vardopoulos, I. (2022). Long-term planning and development for urban and regional inclusion, safety, resilience, and sustainability. Insights from Singapore. Region & Periphery, 14(14), 59–79.

King, R., Proudfoot, L., and Smith, B. (1997). The Mediterranean. Environment and Society. London: Arnold.

Kourliouros, E. (1997). Planning industrial location in greater Athens: The interaction between deindustrialization and anti-industrialism during the 1980s. European Planning Studies, 5(4), 435–460.

Kresl, P. K. (2007). Planning Cities for the Future. The Successes and Failures of Urban Economic Strategies in Europe. Cheltenham: Edward Elgar.

Krumholz, N. (1992). Roman impressions: Contemporary city planning and housing in Rome. Landscape and Urban Planning, 22(2–4), 107–114.

Kuznetsova, O. V. (2019). Settlement transformation and the problems of its adequate consideration in the spatial development strategy. Population and Economics, 3(1), 53–62.

Lambin, E. F., and Meyfroidt, P. (2010). Land use transitions: Socio-ecological feedback versus socio-economic change. Land Use Policy, 27(2), 108–118.

Lambooy, J. G. (1998). Polynucleation and economic development: The Randstad. European Planning Studies, 6(4), 457–467.

Lamonica, G. R., Recchioni, M. C., Chelli, F. M., and Salvati, L. (2020). The efficiency of the cross-entropy method when estimating the technical coefficients of input–output tables. Spatial Economic Analysis, 15(1), 62–91.

Leitner, H., Peck, J., and Sheppard, E. S. (2007). Contesting Neoliberalism: Urban Frontiers. Guilford Press.

Leontidou, L. (1990). The Mediterranean City in Transition. Cambridge: Cambridge University Press.

Leontidou, L. (1996) Alternatives to modernism in (Southern) urban theory: Exploring in-between spaces. International Journal of Urban and Regional Research, 20(2), 180–197.

Li, S., Zhou, C., Wang, S., Gao, S., and Liu, Z. (2019). Spatial Heterogeneity in the Determinants of Urban Form: An Analysis of Chinese Cities with a GWR Approach. Sustainability, 11(2), 479.

Longhi, C., and Musolesi, A. (2007). European cities in the process of economic integration: Towards structural convergence. Annals of Regional Science, 41, 333–351.

Mairota, P., Thornes, J.B., and Geeson, N. (1998). Atlas of Mediterranean environments in Europe. The desertification context. Wiley, Chichester, 205 pp.

Maloutas, T. (2007). Socioeconomic classification models and contextual difference: The "European socioeconomic classes" (ESeC) from a south European angle. South European Society and Politics, 12(4), 443–460.

Manola, M. (2022). Contribution of the Venetian Monuments of Rhodes to Cultural Tourism and the Local Development of the Island. Open Journal for Research in Economics, 5(1), 35–42.

Maravegias, N., and Doukas, Y. E. (2012). A Stategy for Rural Development in Greece: The Case od Island Areas. Region & Periphery, 1, 37.

Mariani, F., Zambon, I., and Salvati, L. (2018). Population matters: Identifying metropolitan sub-centers from diachronic density-distance curves, 1960–2010. Sustainability, 10(12), 46–53.

Maris, G., Sklias, P., and Maravegias, N. (2022). The political economy of the Greek economic crisis in 2020. European Politics and Society, 23(4), 447–467.

Marquard, E., Bartke, S., Gifreu i Font, J., Humer, A., Jonkman, A., Jürgenson, E., Marot, N., Poelmans, L., Repe, B., Rybski, R., Schröter-Schlaack, C., Sobocká, J., Tophøj Sørensen, M., Vejchodská, E., Yiannakou, A., and Bovet, J. (2020). Land Consumption and Land Take: Enhancing Conceptual Clarity for Evaluating Spatial Governance in the EU Context. Sustainability, 12(19), 8269.

Marull, J., and Mallarach, J.M. (2005). A GIS methodology for assessing ecological connectivity: application to Barcelona Metropolitan Area. Landscape and Urban Planning, 71, 243–262.

Marull, J., Pino, J., Tello, E., and Cordobilla, M.J. (2009). Social metabolism, landscape change and land-use planning in the Barcelona Metropolitan Region. Land Use Policy, 27, 497–510.

Masini, E., Tomao, A., Barbati, A., Corona, P., Serra, P., and Salvati, L. (2019). Urban growth, land-use efficiency, and local socioeconomic context: A comparative analysis of 417 metropolitan regions in Europe. Environmental Management, 633, 322–337.

Morrow, N., Salvati, L., Colantoni, A., and Mock, N. (2018). Rooting the future: On-farm trees' contribution to household energy security and asset creation as a resilient development pathway-evidence from a 20-year panel in rural Ethiopia. Sustainability, 10(12), 4716.

Moulaert, F., Rodríguez, A., and Swyngedouw, E. (2003). The Globalized City: Economic Restructuring and Social Polarization in European Cities. Oxford: Oxford University Press.

Munafò, M., Norero, C., Sabbi, A., and Salvati, L. (2010). Soil Sealing in the Growing City: A Survey in Rome, Italy ‡. Scottish Geographical Journal, 126(3), 153–161.

Muñoz, F. (2003). Lock living: Urban sprawl in Mediterranean cities. Cities, 20, 381–385.

Newman, P., and Thornley, A. (2011). Planning World Cities: Globalization and Urban Politics. Macmillan International Higher Education, New York.

Nickayin, S. S., Sateriano, A., Salvia, R., and Salvati, L. (2021). Thirty Years Later: Homage (and Criticism) to Mediterranean Cities. In S. S. Nickain (Ed.), Complexity and Resilience. River Publishers: New York, NY, USA.

Nikolakopoulos, K., Pavlopoulos, K., Chalkias, C., and Manou, D. (2005). Monitoring the urban expansion of Athens using remote sensing and GIS techniques in the last 35 years. Proceedings of SPIE, Vol. 5983.

Orenstein, D. E., Frenkel, A., and Jahshan, F. (2014). Methodology matters: Measuring urban spatial development using alternative methods. Environment and Planning B: Planning and Design, 41(1), 3–23.

Pacione, M. (2003). Urban environmental quality and human wellbeing—a social geographical perspective. Landscape and Urban Planning, 65(1-2), 19–30.

Patacchini, E., and Zenou, Y. (2009). Urban sprawl in Europe. Brookings-Wharton Papers on Urban Affairs, 125–149.

Paul, V., and Tonts, M. (2005). Containing urban sprawl: Trends in land use and spatial planning in the metropolitan region of Barcelona. Journal of Environmental Planning and Management, 48(1), 7–35.

Pelorosso, R., Leone, A., and Boccia, L. 2009. Land cover and land use change in the Italian central Apennines: a comparison of assessment methods. Applied Geography, 29, 35–48.

Perrin, C., Nougarèdes, B., Sini, L., Branduini, P., and Salvati, L. (2018). Governance changes in peri-urban farmland protection following decentralisation: A comparison between Montpellier (France) and Rome (Italy). Land Use Policy, 70, 535–546.

Petrakos, G., Rontos, K., Salvati, L., Vavoura, C., and Vavouras, I. (2023). Income Inequality in the Over-Indebted Eurozone Countries and the Role of the Excessive Deficit Procedure. Open Economies Review.

Phelps, N. A., Parsons, N., Ballas, D., and Dowling, A. (2006). Post-suburban Europe: Planning and Politics at the Margins of Europe's Capital Cities. Basingstoke: Palgrave MacMillan.

Polyzos, S., Christopoulou, O., Minetos, D., and Leal Filho, W. (2008). An overview of urban-rural land use interactions in Greece. International Journal of Agricultural Resources Governance and Ecology, 7(3), 276–296.

Portnov, B. A., and Safriel, U. N. (2004). Combating desertification in the Negev: Dryland agriculture vs. dryland urbanization. Journal of Arid Environments, 56, 659–680.

Prokopová, M., Cudlín, O., Vèeláková, R., Lengyel, S., Salvati, L., and Cudlín, P. (2018). Latent drivers of landscape transformation in Eastern Europe: Past, present and future. Sustainability, 10(8), 2918.

Purcell, M. (2009). Resisting neoliberalisation: Communicative planning or counterhegemonic movements? Planning Theory, 8, 140–165.

Ragazou, K., Passas, I., Garefalakis, A., Zafeiriou, E., and Kyriakopoulos, G. (2022). The Determinants of the Environmental Performance of EU Financial Institutions: An Empirical Study with a GLM Model. Energies, 15(15), 5325.

Ragazou, K., Passas, I., and Garefalakis, A. (2022). It Is Time for Anti-Bribery: Financial Institutions Set the New Strategic "Roadmap" to Mitigate Illicit Practices and Corruption in the Market. Administrative Sciences, 12(4), 166.

Rodrigo-Comino, J., Egidi, G., Sateriano, A., Poponi, S., Mosconi, E. M., and Gimenez Morera, A. (2021). Suburban fertility and metropolitan cycles: Insights from European cities. Sustainability, 13(4), 2181.

Rodríguez-Pose, A., and Storper, M. (2020). Housing, urban growth and inequalities: The limits to deregulation and upzoning in reducing economic and spatial inequality. Urban Studies, 57(2), 223–248.

Rojas, C., Muñiz, I., and Pino, J. (2013). Understanding the Urban Sprawl in the Mid-Size Latin American Cities through the Urban Form: Analysis of the Concepción Metropolitan Area (Chile). Journal of Geographic Information System, 05(03), 222–234.

Rontos, K., Grigoriadis, E., Sateriano, A., Syrmali, M., Vavouras, I., and Salvati, L. (2016). Lost in protest, found in segregation: Divided cities in the light of the 2015 "Oχι" referendum in Greece. City, Culture and Society, 7(3), 139–148.

Rose, D., and Harrison, E. (2014). Social Class in Europe: An Introduction to the European Socio-economic Classification (Vol. 10). Routledge, London.

Sallustio, L., Pettenella, D., Merlini, P., Romano, R., Salvati, L., Marchetti, M., and Corona, P. (2018). Assessing the economic marginality of agricultural lands in Italy to support land use planning. Land Use Policy, 76(2), 526–534.

Salvati, L. (2014). Towards a polycentric region? The socio-economic trajectory of Rome, an 'eternally Mediterranean' city. Tijdschrift voor economische en sociale geografie, 105(3), 268–284.

Salvati, L. (2016). From sprawl to compactness and back: population dynamics (1848–2011) and the economic structure of a Mediterranean city. GeoJournal, 81(2), 319–332.

Salvati, L. (2018). The 'niche' city: A multifactor spatial approach to identify local-scale dimensions of urban complexity. Ecological Indicators, 94(3), 62–73.

Salvati, L. (2019). Farmers and the city: Urban sprawl, socio-demographic polarization and land fragmentation in a mediterranean region, 1961–2009. City, Culture and Society, 18, 1002845.

Salvati, L., and Morelli, V. G. (2014). Unveiling Urban Sprawl in the Mediterranean Region: Towards a Latent Urban Transformation? International Journal of Urban and Regional Research, 38(6), 1935–1953.

Salvati, L., and Carlucci, M. (2011). The economic and environmental performances of rural districts in Italy: Are competitiveness and sustainability compatible targets? Ecological Economics, 70(12), 2446–2453.

Salvati, L., and Carlucci, M. (2016). Patterns of sprawl: The socioeconomic and territorial profile of dispersed urban areas in Italy. Regional Studies, 50(8), 1346–1359.

Salvati, L., Ciommi, M. T., Serra, P., and Chelli, F. M. (2019). Exploring the spatial structure of housing prices under economic expansion and stagnation: The role of socio-demographic factors in metropolitan Rome, Italy. Land Use Policy, 81, 143–152.

Salvati, L., and De Rosa, S. (2014). 'Hidden Polycentrism'or 'Subtle Dispersion'? Urban growth and long-term sub-centre dynamics in three Mediterranean cities. Land Use Policy, 39, 233–243.

Salvati, L., Mavrakis, A., Serra, P., and Carlucci, M. (2015). Lost in translation, found in entropy: An exploratory data analysis of latent growth factors in a Mediterranean city (1960–2010). Applied Geography, 60, 107–119.

Salvati, L., Serra, P., Bencardino, M., and Carlucci, M. (2019). Re-urbanizing the European city: A multivariate analysis of population dynamics during expansion and recession times. European Journal of Population, 35(1), 1–28.

Salvati, L., Zambon, I., Chelli, F. M., and Serra, P. (2018). Do spatial patterns of urbanization and land consumption reflect different socioeconomic contexts in Europe? Science of the Total Environment, 625, 722–730.

Salvati, L., and Zitti, M. (2007). Territorial disparities, natural resource distribution, and land degradation: a case study in southern Europe. Geojournal, 70, 185–194.

Salvati, L., Zitti, M., and Carlucci, M. (2017). In-between regional disparities and spatial heterogeneity: a multivariate analysis of territorial divides in Italy. Journal of Environmental Planning and Management, 60(6), 997–1015.

Salvati, L., Zitti, M., and Sateriano, A. (2013). Changes in the city vertical profile as an indicator of sprawl: Evidence from a Mediterranean region. Habitat International, 38, 119–125.

Salvia, R., Colantoni, A., Bianchini, L., Egidi, G., Polinesi, G., Salvati, L., and Quaranta, G. (2022). 'Old' Territorial Disparities and 'New' Spatial Patterns: Unraveling the Latent Nexus between Sustainable Development and Desertification Risk in Italy. Economies, 10(2), 50.

Salvia, R., Egidi, G., Salvati, L., Rodrigo-Comino, J., and Quaranta, G. (2020). In-Between 'Smart' Urban Growth and 'Sluggish' Rural Development? Reframing Population Dynamics in Greece, 1940–2019. Sustainability, 12(15), 6165.

Salvia, R., Quaranta, V., Sateriano, A., and Quaranta, G. (2022). Land Resource Depletion, Regional Disparities, and the Claim for a Renewed 'Sustainability Thinking'under Early Desertification Conditions. Resources, 11(3), 28.

Salvia, R., Serra, P., Zambon, I., Cecchini, M., and Salvati, L. (2018). In-Between Sprawl and Neo-Rurality: Sparse Settlements and the Evolution of Socio-Demographic Local Context in a Mediterranean Region. Sustainability, 10(10), 3670.

Schneider, A., and Woodcock, C. E. (2008). Compact, dispersed, fragmented, extensive? A comparison of urban growth in twenty-five global cities using remotely sensed data, pattern metrics and census information. Urban Studies, 45(3), 659–692.

Serra, P., Saurí, D., and Salvati, L. (2018). Peri-urban agriculture in Barcelona: outlining landscape dynamics vis-à-vis socio-environmental functions. Landscape Research, 43(5), 613–631.

Seto, K. C., and Kaufmann, R. K. (2003). Modeling the Drivers of Urban Land Use Change in the Pearl River Delta, China: Integrating Remote Sensing with Socioeconomic Data. Land Economics, 79(1), 106–121.

Simmie, J., and Martin, R. (2010). The economic resilience of regions: Towards an evolutionary approach. Cambridge Journal of Regions, Economy and Society, 3(1), 27–43.

Soliman, A.M. (2004). Regional planning scenarios in South Lebanon: the challenge of rural-urban interactions in the era of liberation and globalization. Habitat International, 28, 385–408.

Spindler, C. J., and Forrester, J. P. (1993). Economic Development Policy. Urban Affairs Quarterly, 29(1), 28–53.

Stavroulakis, D., Mitoula, R., Kaldis, P., and Papagrigoriou, A. (2013). Creativity and cultural capital in the Periphery: Evidence from two Greek cities. International Journal of Sustainable Economies Management, 2(2), 48–85.

Tello, E., and Ostos, J. R. (2012). Water consumption in Barcelona and its regional environmental imprint: A long-term history (1717–2008). Regional Environmental Change, 12(2), 347–361.

Terzi, F., and Bolen, F. (2009). Urban sprawl measurement of Istanbul. European Planning Studies, 17(10), 1559–1570.

Tewdwr-Jones, M., and McNeill, D. (2000). The politics of city-region planning and governance: Reconciling the national, regional and urban in the competing voices of institutional restructuring. European Urban and Regional Studies, 7(2), 119–134.

Theobald, D. (2001). Land use dynamics beyond the American urban fringe. Geographical Review, 91(3), 544–564.

Theodoropoulou, H., Vamvakari, M., and Mitoula, R. (2009). Community development in the east prefecture of Attica, Greece, following the 2004 Summer Olympic Games of Athens. International Journal of Sustainable Development and Planning, 4(2), 112–122.

Tomao, A., Quatrini, V., Corona, P., Ferrara, A., Lafortezza, R., and Salvati, L. (2017). Resilient landscapes in Mediterranean urban areas: Understanding factors influencing forest trends. Environmental Research, 156, 1–9.

Tombolini, I., Rodrigo-Comino, J., and Salvati, L. (2022). Mediterranean Europe, a Fragile Landscape: Metropolitan Growth and Urban Sprawl. In I. Tombolini, J. Rodrigo-Comino, and L. Salvati (Eds.), Land Quality and Sustainable Urban Forms. Changing Landscapes and Socioeconomic Structures of European Cities, (pp. 75–103). Springer: Cham, Switzerland.

Torrens, P. M. (2008). A tool kit for measuring sprawl. Applied Spatial Analysis and Policy, 1, 5–36.

Trikalitis, K., and Manola, M. (2023). The Contribution of Religious Monuments to Local and Tourist Development. Open Journal for Research in Economics, 6(1), 35–40.

Tsai, Y. H. (2005). Quantifying urban form: Compactness versus 'sprawl.' Urban Studies, 42(1), 141–161.

Tsilika, E., and Vardopoulos, I. (2022). The FIX-up mix-up; undue façadism or adaptive reuse? Examining the former FIX brewery transformation into the National Museum of Contemporary Art in Athens. Archnet-IJAR: International Journal of Architectural Research, 16(3), 688–709.

Turok, I., and Mykhnenko, V. (2007). The trajectories of European cities, 1960-2005. Cities, 24(3), 165–182.

Vardopoulos, I. (2022). Industrial building adaptive reuse for museum. Factors affecting visitors' perceptions of the sustainable urban development potential. Building and Environment, 222, 109391.

Vardopoulos, I. (2023). Adaptive Reuse for Sustainable Development and Land Use: A Multivariate Linear Regression Analysis Estimating Key Determinants of Public Perceptions. Heritage, 6(2), 809–828.

Vardopoulos, I., Giannopoulos, K., Papaefthymiou, E., Temponera, E., Chatzithanasis, G., Goussia-Rizou, M., Karymbalis, E., Michalakelis, C., Tsartas, P., and Sdrali, D. (2023). Urban buildings sustainable adaptive reuse into tourism accommodation establishments: a SOAR analysis. Discover Sustainability, 4(1), 50.

Vardopoulos, I., Ioannides, S., Georgiou, M., Voukkali, I., Salvati, L., and Doukas, Y. E. (2023). Shaping sustainable cities: A long-rerm GIS-emanated spatial analysis of settlement growth and planning in a coastal Mediterranean European city. Sustainability, 15(14), 11202.

Vardopoulos, I., Stamopoulos, C., Chatzithanasis, G., Michalakelis, C., Giannouli, P., and Pastrapa, E. (2020). Considering urban development paths and processes on account of adaptive reuse projects. Buildings, 10(4), 73.

Vardopoulos, I., Tsilika, E., Sarantakou, E., Zorpas, A. A., Salvati, L., and Tsartas, P. (2021). An integrated SWOT-PESTLE-AHP model assessing sustainability in adaptive reuse projects. Applied Sciences, 11(15), 7134.

Vasta, Figueiredo, Valente, Vihinen, and Nieto-Romero. (2019). Place-Based Policies for Sustainability and Rural Development: The Case of a Portuguese Village "Spun" in Traditional Linen. Social Sciences, 8(10), 289.

Vidal, M., Domènech, E., and Saurí, D. (2011). Changing geographies of water-related consumption: Residential swimming pools in suburban Barcelona. Area, 43(1), 67–75.

Vinci, S., and Salvati, L. (2022). Strategic Management of Sustainable Urban Development: Economic Downturns, Metropolitan Governance and Local Communities. CRC Press: Boca Raton, Florida, USA.

Vinci, S., Egidi, G., Salvia, R., Gimenez Morera, A., and Salvati, L. (2022). Natural population growth and urban management in metropolitan regions: Insights from pre-crisis and post-crisis Athens, Greece. Urban Studies, 59(12), 2527–2544.

Vinci, S., Vardopoulos, I., and Salvati, L. (2023). A tale of a shrinking City? Exploring the complex interplay of socio-demographic dynamics in the recent development of Attica, Greece. Cities, 132, 104089.

Wang, S., Yang, Z., and Liu, H. (2011). Impact of urban economic openness on real estate prices: Evidence from thirty-five cities in China. China Economic Review, 22(1), 42–54.

Weber, C., Petropoulou, C., and Hirsch, J. (2005). Urban development in the Athens metropolitan area using remote sensing data with supervised analysis and GIS. International Journal of Remote Sensing, 26, 785–796.

Xu, C., Haase, D., Su, M., Wang, Y., and Pauleit, S. (2020). Assessment of landscape changes under different urban dynamics based on a multiple-scenario modeling approach. Environment and Planning B: Urban Analytics and City Science, 47(8), 1361–1379.

Zambon, I., and Salvati, L. (2019). Metropolitan growth, urban cycles and housing in a Mediterranean country, 1910s–2010s. Cities, 95, 102412.

Zambon, I., Benedetti, A., Ferrara, C., and Salvati, L. (2018). Soil matters? A multivariate analysis of socioeconomic constraints to urban expansion in Mediterranean Europe. Ecological Economics, 146, 173–183.

Zambon, I., Colantoni, A., and Salvati, L. (2019). Horizontal vs vertical growth: Understanding latent patterns of urban expansion in large metropolitan regions. Science of the Total Environment, 654, 778–785.

Zambon, I., Serra, P., Sauri, D., Carlucci, M., and Salvati, L. (2017). Beyond the 'Mediterranean city': socioeconomic disparities and urban sprawl in three Southern European cities. Geografiska Annaler: Series B, Human Geography, 99(3), 319–337.

Zitti, M., Zambon, I., Mavrakis, A., and Salvati, L. (2018). The Way Toward Dispersed Metropolitan Growth: Land-use Efficiency and the Abandonment of a Mediterranean Compact Tradition. International Journal of Ecology and Development, 33(1), 108–124.

2

Whispers of Change: Thirty Years for Redefining the "Mediterranean City"

Francisco Escrivà Saneugenio, Adele Sateriano, Luca Salvati, and Ioannis Vardopoulos

Envisioning a radical shift in the definitions of "periphery" and "center," along with fundamental reconceptualizations of "urban" and "metropolitan," "Mediterranean" paradigms examined the intricacies of cities and regions through a dual perspective of "global" and "local" lenses (Minca, 2004). The term "Mediterranean city," often seen as an instance of "forced taxonomies" in geographical and sociological literature, presented itself as a deliberate counterpoint to prevailing Anglo-American models of urban development (Leontidou, 1990; Carlucci, 2017). This approach prompted a post-modern reinterpretation of the concept, responding to recent critiques of traditional urban theories and fostering a multidisciplinary dialogue across geographical, demographic, and economic domains (D'Agata, 2024). This stance occasionally challenged a metaphorical vision prevalent in discussions about Mediterranean urbanity (Braudel, 1987).

Over three decades have elapsed since Lila Leontidou's seminal work, "The Mediterranean city in transition." The Mediterranean region has hosted two Olympic Games – in Barcelona (1992) and Athens (2004) – as well as significant events like Expo 1998 in Lisbon, the 2000 Jubilee in Rome, and sporting spectacles in Valencia and Thessaloniki (Panagiotopoulos, 2023). These cities, among others, have been the focal points of numerous studies, contributing to the ongoing academic discourse on "Mediterranean typologies" of cities. Despite Barcelona's acclaim as "the coolest city in Europe" since the early 1990s, the scholarly conversation persists.

The renewed interest in Mediterranean urbanities has generated a substantial body of research, with a particular focus on individual cities such as Barcelona, Istanbul, Athens, Lisbon, Madrid, Seville, Thessaloniki, Valencia, and, to a lesser extent, Rome and Naples. Recent empirical investigations have provided insights into the complex interplay between spatial planning and informal growth, recontextualizing the long-term trajectory of Southern Europe (Benevolo 1990; Kourliouros 1997; Dal Pozzolo 2002; Coccossis *et al.* 2005).

Quest for the Essence: Unraveling the Tapestry of "Mediterranean Urbanity"

The discourse on the recent evolution of Mediterranean cities is intricately linked to a broader dialogue on the Mediterranean as a political arena for urban and regional development (Theodora, 2020; Salvati, 2014). The challenge lies in elusive definitions, ambiguous boundaries, diverse cultures, and finely detailed territories, making the reflection on the "Mediterranean region" both intricate and kaleidoscopic (Matvejevic, 1996, 1998). Crafting an operational definition for the "Mediterranean region," as Conti and Segre (1998) propose, requires proof of the existence of a unique Mediterranean scale capable of analyzing physical boundaries encapsulating homogeneous socioeconomic processes (Leontidou, 1990, 1993). From this standpoint, the paths of Mediterranean urbanization emerge as complex dynamics grounded in adaptable concepts (Figure 2.1), with territorial extension subject to variation based on academic perspectives (Vaiou, 2004).

This critical perspective diverges from a traditional "reductionist" approach by: (i) advocating for an evaluation grounded in the distinctive characteristics of Mediterranean urban systems (Salvati, 2014; Feleki, 2018), (ii) rejecting economic interpretations based on the "convergence" paradigm (Konchak and Pascual, 2006), (iii) providing a critical assessment of the dichotomy between urban culture and regional economic structures (Ward and Jonas, 2004; Doukas, 2023), and (iv) initiating a broader discourse on sustainable development paths incorporating additional components (territorial, ecological, planning, and policy) into the "growth" debate (Leontidou, 2003; D'Agata, 2023).

Despite the gradual transition of certain Mediterranean cities toward more "conventional" metropolitan structures and urban models integrated into the global economy, the critical perspective of a "Mediterranean way" to urbanization remains applicable in transitional contexts undergoing structural crises (Leontidou, 2014). Summarizing this view, Minca (2003) envisions the Mediterranean region as a nebula comprising a series of virtual networks and materials that interconnect information, people, services, and goods across various places and nodes (Figure 2.2). These interactions possess an only seemingly ephemeral dimension, intrinsically detached from the linear logic

Figure 2.1 The Mirable "complexity" of the Mediterranean "tapestry": mixing compact settlements and a traditional rural area, downtown Granada and the Huerta, Spain. Source: Authors' photographic archive.

underlying the measurement and interpretation of economic space and its associated social context – a concept analogous to what we refer to as "territory" (Vaiou, 1997).

With this viewpoint in mind, criticism emerges against schematic approaches characterizing positivistic interpretations and the (presumed) "geometry" and "linearity" of the reciprocal relationship between society and territory (Salvati *et al.*, 2014). This critique challenges the backdrop that solely focuses on a quantitative understanding of local development processes (Vinci *et al.*, 2023). By questioning the scale of economic production as a foundational criterion for interpreting urban phenomena (Lemonakis, 2023), we discern that the ambiguity and non-linearity inherent in the Mediterranean region constitute its wealth and strength rather than weaknesses and inconsistencies (Minca, 2004). From this perspective, Mediterranean spaces should not be labeled as "disadvantaged," "depressed," "marginal," "uncompetitive," or lacking "international credibility" and "national visibility." These spaces are inherently challenging to define uniformly and distinctly due to the

Figure 2.2 Social mixes reflected in downtown settlements, central Lisbon. Source: Authors' photographic archive.

spatial logic employing binary criteria of inclusion/ exclusion and the pervasive "linear thinking" dominating academic discourse (Salvati, 2018). Linear approaches and interpretative frameworks have underpinned this exclusionary logic within the framework of a "reductionist," largely unremarkable interpretation of Mediterranean urbanities (Kayser, 1996).

It is posited that approaches employing both narrative and quantitative tools can significantly contribute to the interpretation of complex socioeconomic systems (see Vardopoulos and Konstantinou, 2017). While acknowledging the role of statistics and indicators in understanding the functional and structural characteristics of "southern urbanities," there is an ongoing search for a more empirical foundation rooted in narratives, metaphors, images,

Figure 2.3 The "metaphoric" landscape of contemporary cities in the Mediterranean; Naples in-between the sea and the mountains inland. Source: Authors' photographic archive.

horizons, maps, and flexible boundaries (Vinci *et al.*, 2023). In practice, statistics appear insufficient when assessing latent growth factors that are inherently challenging to identify and measure (Salvati *et al.*, 2018). Despite the extensive body of research on Mediterranean geographies (Matvejevic, 1996), assuming the Mediterranean region as a homogeneous space is deemed a misleading inference (Salvati. 2020). Engaging with narratives, metaphors, and discourses allows for a nuanced understanding of a boundary-less, more permeable, and largely heterogeneous space (Figure 2.3).

"Southern Urbanity," a Key Trait of Mediterranean Development

A comprehensive understanding of the "Mediterranean discourse," rich in ambiguities and evocations, warrants the abandonment of the "stiffness of deterministic constructs" (Bromberger, 2006). Diminishing the influence of functionalist discourses and envisioning a heterotopic space, akin to an ongoing utopia, involves recognizing a captivating space that not only establishes order but also sets the stage for its complete deconstruction (Minca, 2004). Contemplating the Mediterranean Sea as a heterotopia offers the potential for a definition largely unaffected by determinism and functionalism (Farinelli, 1998). In regional analyses of Southern Europe, the focus has traditionally been on lowlands, perceived as opportunities for human settlement and outcomes of public policy planning, particularly starting from the sea coast (Giannakourou, 2005). Cities interrupt the homogeneity of agricultural and

Figure 2.4 Unraveling the stratification of socioeconomic forces along the Mediterranean fringes; peri-urban vineyards and the background dispersed city in-between Rome and Tivoli, Italy. Source: Authors' own elaboration.

forest low-populated landscapes (Figure 2.4), determining a "jump scale," which is not associated with demographic and economic disparities only but reflects an intimately polarized landscape (Medley *et al.*, 1995; Doukas *et al.*, 2022). The Mediterranean region thus reflects a "geography of the fracture" (Kayser, 1996). Developed areas diverged from emerging and disadvantaged districts thanks to the strength of some commercial and industrial cities against the weakness of rural landscapes (Hall and Pain, 2006; Maravegias and Doukas, 2012).

This deterministic perspective receives only partial affirmation in the transition toward polycentric models in geography (Davoudi, 2003). The global standing of countries surrounding the Mediterranean, marked by an unstable role in economic global systems (Vinci *et al.*, 2023), unresolved environmental challenges (Vardopoulos *et al.*, 2018), pronounced regional disparities (Xanthos *et al.*, 2022), and escalating social instability (Passas *et al.*, 2022), continues to perpetuate their "peripheral" status today (Economou, 1997). Farinelli (1998) contemplated the characterization of the "peripheral" Mediterranean as a region marked by political turbulence, economic and social instability, secularism, and religious traditionalism. This constraint extends beyond the economic realm, underscoring the imperative to restructure urban research within complex territorial systems (Deffontaines, 1972).

The economic underdevelopment of the Mediterranean region has been thoroughly explored in earlier works (Leontidou, 1993; Farinelli, 1998; Minca, 2004). These studies have challenged the metaphorical connotations of "backwardness," advocating for a more "positivistic" term, such as the concept of "other modernity." This notion refers to a condition of modernity that defies strict quantification using exclusively quantitative criteria. The thought-provoking idea of "resistance to modernity" has also been incorporated into this discourse. It represents the articulation of critical perspectives diverging from the dominant Anglo-American culture, expressing a nuanced impatience with the rules, identity, and objective criteria characteristic of specific regional contexts (Leontidou, 1995).

These contributions unveil the limitations of positivist definitions. Minca contends that the Mediterranean region defies reduction to a singular mechanistic metaphor, rejecting the narrative of fallback positions and economic backwardness. He calls upon scholars to engage in a personal and subjective elaboration of narrative spaces, borders, and horizons, transcending the supposedly ordered and linear patterns associated with European identity (Beriatos and Gospodini, 2004). Reinterpreting the distinctive characteristics of Mediterranean peripheries emerges as a pertinent task within regional science (Manola, 2022). This entails not merely seeking alternative definitions, measurements, and concepts but underscores the imperative of reinstating crucial issues like the centrality of territories, local communities, and regional economic systems into cultural and political agendas (LeGates and Stout, 1996).

Conversely, the Mediterranean has recently reclaimed, at least partially, its cultural and social centrality between Europe, Africa, and the Middle East (Knapp and Dommelen, 2010). Post-crisis economic scenarios and geopolitical uncertainty contribute to an inherent redefinition of this central role in the global hierarchy (Lemonakis *et al.*, 2023). Certain regions, particularly those most open to trade, have strategically positioned themselves to regain prominence in the global context (Vardopoulos *et al.*, 2023). This dimension aligns with intervention policies for Mediterranean development that strongly emphasize strengthening the role of cities (Salvatori, 2008). Historically, cities have served as bastions of economic growth and social and cultural structures capable of ensuring employment and prosperity, embodying dynamic and productive territories (Reeder and Rodger, 2001). Mediterranean cities are also striving to recreate the allure and ambiance that attract tourists worldwide (Karytsas *et al.*, 2019), seeking an image that is not only pleasant, efficient, and vibrant but also rich in history and culture (Delladetsima, 2006). Many of these cities, in tandem with the opportunities presented by

Figure 2.5 Tourism development in the outer fringe of Malaga, Spain. Source: Authors' own elaboration.

globalization (Vardopoulos, 2022), have long been working to consolidate or enhance their position in the continental tourism hierarchy (Vardopoulos *et al.*, 2023) (Figure 2.5).

Urban Centralities and the Mediterranean Periphery

The revival of urban centrality has been fortified through a strategy entailing projects structured over time (Vicino *et al.*, 2007). Nonetheless, the gradual decline of certain Mediterranean cities since the sixteenth century is rooted in the development of commercial, productive, social, and cultural networks that have shifted progressively toward North America, Northern Europe, and the East (Ciommi *et al.*, 2022). This backdrop reflects economically weakened territories but with notable instances of vitality and convergence (Figure 2.6). Another enduring centrality in the Mediterranean can be traced in the tourism sector (Karytsas *et al.*, 2019). However, territorial disparities between countries manifest in this sector concerning infrastructure, accommodation, and environmental impacts (Vardopoulos *et al.*, 2023). These disparities stem from the concentration of local infrastructure, the (limited) quality of human capital employed, and the absence of alternative and innovative hospitality (Troin, 1997).

Figure 2.6 The economic centrality of Mediterranean cities, downtown Seville and the countryside, Spain. Source: Authors' photographic archive.

The swift population expansion is a distinct characteristic of the Mediterranean city and represents another hallmark of the region (Vinci *et al.*, 2023). The factors influencing urban growth, observed at least until the 1990s along the north bank and still exerting influence on the south bank, are effectively encapsulated by Ludlow (1994). The urbanization process, catalyzed by rural transformation and propelled by particular (land/ housing) pricing policies, leads to the disproportionate growth of cities (Davis and Henderson, 2003; Doukas, 2011). This surge in population has confronted Mediterranean urban regions with novel and pressing challenges (Figure 2.7), notably the environmental ramifications of this substantial rural exodus (Vardopoulos, 2022).

The ecological challenges stemming from urbanization intertwine with those arising from the swift conversion of agricultural land into artificial spaces (Doukas *et al.*, 2022). These landscapes, ecologically fragile, become susceptible to environmental pressures that can trigger destructive cycles, fostering deforestation, desertification, and the irreversible depletion of natural capital in a broad context (Kayser 1996; Escolano *et al.*, 2018). Coupled with demographic shifts and undeniable cultural transformations, the pronounced transition of production activities from an industrial economy to (more or less) advanced services constitutes another hallmark of Mediterranean urban development (Vinci *et al.*, 2023). This transformation, in itself, is not exclusive to the Mediterranean basin. It would be more insightful to examine the trajectory of this phenomenon in Mediterranean European cities, probing the

Figure 2.7 Informal sprawl, late industrialization, and the rural gap in Acharnes, Northern Athens. Source: Authors' photographic archive.

significance of advanced services – as an indicator of urban competitiveness – in the local economy (Melendez-Pastor *et al.*, 2017).

The partial ineffectiveness of development policies aimed at modernization, competitiveness, and the rejuvenation of Central Business Districts has been instrumental in sustaining ongoing processes of urban expansion (Edgington, 1982). Mediterranean informality, indeed, embodies a dualistic perspective (see Tsilika, 2021) involving (i) widespread acknowledgment of the role of markets and capital and (ii) a rejection of the state as a regulatory force in these dynamics (Leontidou, 2014). According to Pace (1996), "in this context, the rule becomes the informal sector rather than the legal economy. The rule does not allow the emergence of a strong middle class and produces workers in the informal sector rather than the proletariat (Torisu, 2006). Late industrialization highlights the absence of 'bourgeois hegemony,' but also the diversity, versatility, and distinctiveness of Mediterranean societies" (Figure 2.7). The foundation of social control facilitating such amalgamation is the supremacy of the family over the state, prioritizing particular interests over the common good (Tsoulouvis, 1996).

"Southern Echoes": The Soul of Mediterranean Urban Development

Grounded in these considerations, Mediterranean urban geographies can be encapsulated by a few significant keywords, creating a feasible framework for

Table 2.1 Interpreting Mediterranean urbanities through spatial scales and the related keywords.

Urban	Regional	National	International
Form	Transition	Governance	Ranking
Cycle	Contrasts	System	Convergence
Segregation	Spillover	Opportunity	Competition
Creativity	Planning	Polycentrism	Synergy
Events	Networks	Polarizations	Globalization

Source: Authors' own elaboration of literature review.

distinguishing and classifying the scale of representation for these phenomena (Feleki *et al.*, 2018; Stratigea *et al.*, 2017). Local contexts, regional patterns, and national/international dimensions emerge as crucial factors when dissecting – and ideally validating – the "Mediterranean city" stereotype (Feleki *et al.*, 2018; Salvati, 2014). At each level of analysis, specific research dimensions warrant emphasis (see Table 2.1). Morphological and functional characteristics of any city, encompassing form, demographic trends, as well as horizontal/vertical social segregation, coupled with the impact of cultural events in fostering urban competitiveness, sustainable planning, and "creative" models, are thoroughly explored (Scott, 2001).

The regional dimension encapsulates the discourse on the transition from compact to sprawling cities, delineating the ongoing evolution of the interplay between urban and rural areas (Delgado-Viñas and Gómez-Moreno, 2022). At this scale, sprawl is contextualized within a framework of polycentric development, wherein sustainable resource management and planning encompass decision spaces on a regional scale (D'Agata *et al.*, 2024). The national scale underscores the uniqueness of most urban systems, conceived as individual "city-state" experiences, evolving through a process of mutual recognition between cities and states (Robinson, 2002). An examination of the international role of Mediterranean cities enriches the proposed interpretative approach (Vardopoulos *et al.*, 2023), emphasizing the commitment of many urban areas to a convergence process toward more competitive, equitable, and sustainably developed futures, challenging the *cliché* of backwardness and informality (Maloutas and Karadimitriou, 2001).

By intertwining economics, geography, and social issues, the intricacies of Mediterranean cities, though challenging to quantify, have consistently drawn the attention of urban analyses, positing Mediterranean cities as the cradle of an advanced urban civilization and cultural tradition rooted in a well-established "astifilia" (Leontidou, 2003). The pursuit of a singular taxonomy for Mediterranean cities has captivated scholars and practitioners

Figure 2.8 "Southern Echoes" and the Mediterranean landscape; upper left: Geronimos monastery in Granada, Spain, at dusk; upper right: burnt uplands in front of Tyrrhenian Sea in Messina, Italy; lower left: a public space along the beach of Daimus, Spain; lower middle: the magnificence of Mole Antonelliana in downtown Turin, Italy; lower right: just the sea, Elafonisos, Greece. Source: Authors' photographic archive.

alike (Salvati, 2014). While selecting specific variable targets might offer some utility for comparison when assuming the urban context as a benchmark (Figure 2.8), adding one more element to these contexts, namely the "good practice" to emulate in the realms of architecture (Tsilika, 2017), planning (Kempton *et al.*, 2022), and the economy (D'Agata *et al.*, 2024), could be misleading, despite its widespread adoption (Pace, 1996).

The pervasive temptation to force Mediterranean urbanities into a kind of "certified copy" of the North has denied cultural traditions, unique urban landscapes, and traditional social practices (Muscarà, 1986). In this vein, the "Mediterranean urban paradigm," evolving through a myriad of concepts and definitions that blend tradition and post-modernism, has purposefully distanced itself from a linear interpretation of the relationships between northern and southern urbanities (Leontidou, 1996). The substantial contribution of Greek, Spanish, and Portuguese scholars, accompanied by numerous voices from Italy and interventions from the southern shores of the Mediterranean, remains significant and resonates in urban geography as the twentieth century drew to a close (Stott *et al.*, 2005).

The debate incorporates an element tied to the concept of post-modernity as expressed by the Mediterranean city – a condition that Leontidou (1993) articulates as a "reaction to modernity." This stance has given rise to a new modernity, seen as a cultural alternative to traditional modernism, critiquing European centralism and the "one-way" vision characteristic of the American world. The transition to the new millennium has, on the one hand, fostered a renewed awareness of urban Mediterranean issues through the ongoing systematization of concepts and urban taxonomies. On the other hand, recent years have witnessed a reorientation of the disciplinary debate toward new currents of thought, more inclined toward polycentric socioeconomic models (Carlucci *et al.*, 2017).

The shift toward a more balanced urban development has also been influenced by literature on the organization and evolution of "global city regions" (Scott, 2001), seen as exemplars of modernity, efficiency, and competitiveness (Lemonakis *et al.*, 2023). The "creative cities" paradigm has further contributed to the emergence of alternative lines of interpretation, challenging the paradigm of the traditional and stereotypical Mediterranean city (Vardopoulos *et al.*, 2023).

The spotlight has turned to the large- and medium-sized cities of Southern Europe – morphologically distinct from the "global city-regions" outlined in Anglophone literature (Tumpel-Gugerell and Mooslechner, 2003), deviating from traditional mono-centric and hyper-compact models (Longhi and Musolesi, 2007). They emerge as protagonists of a polycentric model, at times incipient and in many cases still in its infancy, but poised to become a focal point for future studies on southern urban development (D'Agata *et al.*, 2024). The role of Mediterranean cities in this new discourse, as their urban regions align – partially or entirely – with current trends in "northern" countries, has been the focus of recent research (Salvati and Morelli, 2014). Questions of convergence or divergence, adaptation or resilience, are the emerging themes to explore from various perspectives (Figure 2.9). The future trajectories of Mediterranean cities, the unfolding scenarios for their urban regions in the global market context, architectural landmarks, cultural events, and planning guided by common, albeit varying, rules across European countries remain open for examination (Salvati, 2014).

In pursuit of answers to these intricate questions, a conceptual framework has been outlined in the preceding paragraphs to decipher the socioeconomic conditions, as well as territorial and environmental dimensions, characterizing

Figure 2.9 Before growth: recovering the "essence" of the Mediterranean peri-urban landscape; Vouliagmenis' beach, Southern Athens, at the end of the nineteenth century. Source: Adaptation on public archives' photographs.

the processes of urbanization that have defined Mediterranean urban areas in the most recent period. Mediterranean cities undergo transformation and evolution, reasserting their value and centrality in a world increasingly shaped by networks rather than states and regions (Salvati and Vardopoulos, 2024). Positioned between the global cities of the North and the disadvantaged cities of the South, the Mediterranean city should not be perceived as a formal paradigm of analysis but as a crucial point of distinction in the comparative analysis of diverse urban trajectories, within a backdrop of regional heterogeneity and urban specificity (Balta, 1992). In this context, the comparison among cities, regions, and urban systems to identify archetypes of "Mediterranean" traits serves the purpose of a comprehensive definition of the "Mediterranean city" archetype. This involves delineating a spectrum of potential alternative trajectories, grounded in statistical, empirical, and quantitative criteria, as well as qualitative, perceptual, and emotional assets (Minca, 2004).

Preserving the Past, Shaping the Future: A Sustainable Odyssey in Mediterranean Cities

Identifying distinctive characteristics that uniquely define a prototype of "Mediterranean cities" can be approached through both morphological criteria (*e.g.*, the shape of a city or metropolitan area, the interplay between settlement compactness and population density, and urban growth dynamics across time and space) and functional aspects such as demographic traits of the resident population, intrinsic features of local job markets, well-being and poverty, and processes of social (class and ethnic) segregation (Di Feliciantonio and Salvati, 2014). Suburbanization introduces new perspectives for analysis, embedding the concept of the "Mediterranean city" in vivid images of the "lock living" architectural style and the consequent evolution of lifestyles and consumption, as envisaged by Munoz (2003) in the recent development of Barcelona's fringe. Social changes in suburban Barcelona were interpreted as a consequence of never-ending urban expansion, resulting in settlements dominated by villas, private gardens, and swimming pools surrounded by hyper-controlled and almost fortified residential estates. This landscape progressively adheres to a "territorial model" closely resembling what has long been observed in the North American fringe, with low-density settlements physically disconnected from downtowns.

Simultaneously, several Mediterranean cities still conform to a more generic and undefined model characteristic of the "unrested metropolis under continuous transition" (Leontidou, 2003). Qualifying pre-Olympics Athens' growth as a category of spontaneity *à la* Gramsci, Leontidou envisaged sprawl as a consequence of a socially unbalanced landscape, perhaps unique in Europe. From a distinctly morphological perspective, Mediterranean cities can be viewed as land-saving organisms, adopting efficient decisions in the use of land at the core of compact settlements' development (European Environment Agency, 2006; Zitti *et al.*, 2018). Nevertheless, numerous European Mediterranean cities have gradually shifted toward sprawled models that expand into, and consume, an even larger amount of fertile rural land (Lagarias and Sayas, 2018). Will Southern European cities preserve their distinctive historical centers, consistently attracting masses of tourists and new residents, or will they experience population decline, altering commuter flows and international immigration patterns? Will they move toward more balanced and sustainable models by addressing the longstanding socioeconomic polarization in urban and suburban districts? Will they persist in consuming the surrounding open spaces, developing vacant land even in the presence of crucial historical, cultural, and natural elements warranting protection?

In addressing these questions, consideration was given to local development in the Mediterranean region as a powerful driver of spatial imbalances (Zuindeau, 2007). Economic polarization, a shortage of public housing, the concentration of activities in urban areas coupled with rapid population growth (Figure 2.10), have given rise to noteworthy disparities between cities and the surrounding regions, which struggled to adapt to these transitions

Figure 2.10 Vacant land in rural districts waiting for economic speculation and real estate development; Megara, Western Attica, Greece. Source: Authors' photographic archive.

(Fuschi, 2008). The emergence of externalities related to structure, infrastructure, human, and financial capital has resulted in significant environmental imbalances, depletion of natural resources, habitat fragmentation, and a pervasive loss of biodiversity (Papamichael *et al.*, 2023).

In the wake of the economic and environmental convergence characterizing Southern European regions' shift toward advanced models, a profound "cultural transition" unfolds – a departure from the conventional perception of homogeneous Mediterranean cities. This transformative journey illuminates diverse development paths, particularly on the "European" side, necessitating targeted interventions in transport, air quality, waste management, and urban rejuvenation. Simultaneously, urgent policies are imperative on the southern front to address the surging housing demand and stabilize migration flows. In this dynamic landscape, networking, the exchange of practical experiences, and the honing of planning skills become invaluable tools. The very essence of the "Mediterranean city" is undergoing a metamorphosis, demanding a multidisciplinary approach. It is through the implementation of these multi-dimensional planning strategies that an authentic contribution to the development of Mediterranean cities amidst contemporary challenges is achievable.

Standing on the precipice of the next chapter, the narrative unfolds, beckoning a tapestry to be woven that harmonizes architecture, social life, and the environment – a tale of resilience, adaptation, and vibrant urban futures.

The evolving concept of the "Mediterranean city" challenges one to think beyond traditional boundaries, prompting a nuanced exploration of interconnected urban elements. This narrative is not just about cities; it is about crafting living, breathing entities that reflect the pulse of a region – the heartbeat of a civilization navigating the complexities of the twenty-first century. In contemplating this odyssey, one recognizes that the future trajectory of Mediterranean cities lies in our ability to balance progress with preservation, to navigate urban complexities while cherishing the cultural richness embedded in every cobblestone. This is not merely a conclusion; it is an invitation to an ongoing dialogue – a dialogue that shapes the very fabric of our urban landscapes, encouraging us to envision, adapt, and co-create a Mediterranean urban future that transcends the conventional and embraces the extraordinary.

References

Alaimo, L. S., Ciommi, M., Vardopoulos, I., Nosova, B., and Salvati, L. (2022). The Medium-Term Impact of the COVID-19 Pandemic on Population Dynamics: The Case of Italy. Sustainability, 14(21), 13995.

Allen, J., Barlow, J., Leal, J., Maloutas, T., and Padovan, L. (2004). Housing in Southern Europe. London, UK: Blackwell.

Andersson, R., Quigley J. M., and Wilhelmsson, M. (2005). Agglomeration and the spatial distribution of creativity. Papers in Regional Science, 84(3), 445–464.

Angel, S., Parent, J., Civco, D. L., Blei, A., and Potere, D. (2011). The dimensions of global urban expansion: Estimates and projections for all countries, 2000–2050. Progress in Planning, 75, 53–107.

Arapoglou, V. P., and Sayas, J. (2009). New facets of urban segregation in southern Europe—gender, migration and social class change in Athens. European Urban and Regional Studies, 16(4), 345–362.

Bagavos, C., Verropoulou, G., and Tsimbos, C. (2018). Assessing the contribution of foreign women to period fertility in Greece, 2004–2012. Population, 73(1), 115–130.

Balta P. (1992). La Méditerranée réinventée. La Découverte, Parigi.

Barbieri, P., Bozzon, R., Scherer, S., Grotti, R., and Lugo, M. (2015). The rise of a Latin model? Family and fertility consequences of employment instability in Italy and Spain. European Societies, 17(4), 423–446.

Batty, M., and Longley, P. A. (1994). Fractal cities: a geometry of form and function. Academic press.

Bayona-Carrasco, J., and Gil-Alonso, F. (2012). Suburbanisation and international immigration: The case of the Barcelona Metropolitan Region

(1998–2009). Tijdschrift voor Economische en Sociale Geographie, 103(3), 312–329.
Benevolo L. (1990). Storia della città Europea. Laterza, Bari.
Beriatos, E., and Gospodini, A. (2004). "Glocalising" urban landscapes: Athens and the 2004 Olympics. Cities, 21(3), 187–202.
Bianchini, L., Marucci, A., Sateriano, A., Di Stefano, V., Alemanno, R., and Colantoni, A. (2021). Urbanization and long-term forest dynamics in a metropolitan region of southern Europe (1936–2018). Sustainability, 13(21), 12164.
Billari, F. C., Kohler, H.-P., Andersson, G., and Lundström, H. (2007). Approaching the limit: Long-term trends in late and very late fertility. Population and Development Review, 33, 149–170.
Bocquier, P., and Bree, S. (2018). A regional perspective on the economic determinants of urban transition in 19th-century France. Demographic Research, 38, 1535–1576.
Bocquier, P., and Costa, R. (2015). Which transition comes first? Urban and demographic transitions in Belgium and Sweden. Demographic Research, 33, 1297–1332.
Bongaarts, J., and Watkins, S.C. (1996). Social Interactions and Contemporary Fertility Transitions. Population and Development Review, 22(4), 639–682.
Boyle P. (2003). Population geography: does geography matter in fertility research? Progress in Human Geography, 27(5), 615–626.
Braudel F. (1987). Il Mediterraneo. Bompiani, Milano.
Brodmann, S., Esping-Andersen, G., and Güell, M. (2007). When Fertility is Bargained: Second Births in Denmark and Spain. European Sociological Review, 23(5), 599–613.
Bruegmann, R. (2005). Sprawl: a compact history. Chicago, US: University of Chicago Press.
Buckley, C. (1998). Rural/urban differentials in demographic processes: The Central Asian states. Population Research and Policy Review 17(1), 71–89.
Burgel, G. (2004). Athènes, de la balkanisation à la mondialisation. Méditerranée, 103(3–4), 59–63.
Burger, M., and Meijers, E. (2012). Form follows function? Linking morphological and functional polycentricity. Urban Studies, 49(5), 1127–1149.
Burillo, P., Salvati, L., Matthews, S. A., and Benassi, F. (2020). Local-Scale Fertility Variations in a Low-Fertility Country: Evidence from Spain (2002–2017). Canadian Studies in Population, 47(4), 279–295.
Butler, D. (2004). The fertility riddle. Nature, 432, 38–39.

Buzar, S., Ogden, P. E., and Hall, R. (2005). Households matter: the quiet demography of urban transformation. Progress in Human Geography, 29(4), 413–436.

Cabral, P., Augusto, G., Tewolde, M., and Araya, Y. (2013). Entropy in Urban Systems. Entropy, 15(12), 5223–5236.

Cabré, A. (2003). Facts and Factors on Low Fertility in Southern Europe. The Case of Spain. Journal of Population and Social Security (Population), Supplement to Volume, 1(1), 309–321.

Caldwell, J. C. (2006). Demographic transition theory. Berlin: Springer.

Caldwell, J. C., and Schindlmayr, T. (2003). Explanations of the fertility crisis in modern societies: A search for commonalities. Population Studies, 57(3), 241–263.

Caltabiano, M., Castiglioni, M., and Rosina, A. (2009). Lowest-low fertility: Signs of a recovery in Italy? Demographic Research, 21, 681–718.

Carbonaro, C., Leanza, M., McCann, P., and Medda, F. (2018). Demographic decline, population aging, and modern financial approaches to urban policy. International Regional Science Review, 41(2), 210–232.

Carlucci, M., Chelli, F. M., and Salvati, L. (2018). Toward a new cycle: Short-term population dynamics, gentrification, and re-urbanization of Milan (Italy). Sustainability, 10(9), 3014.

Carlucci, M., Grigoriadis, E., Rontos, K., and Salvati, L. (2017). Revisiting a hegemonic concept: Long-term 'Mediterranean urbanization' in between city re-polarization and metropolitan decline. Applied Spatial Analysis and Policy, 10(3), 347–362.

Cassiers, T., and Kesteloot, C. (2012). Socio-spatial Inequalities and Social Cohesion in European Cities. Urban Studies, 49(9), 1909–1924.

Castro, M. C. (2007). Spatial demography: an opportunity to improve policy making at diverse decision levels. Population Research and Policy Review, 26(5–6), 477–509.

Catalán, B., Sauri, D., and Serra, P. (2008). Urban sprawl in the Mediterranean? Patterns of growth and change in the Barcelona Metropolitan Region 1993–2000. Landscape and Urban Planning, 85(3–4), 174–184.

Cazzola, A., Pasquini, L., and Angeli, A. (2016). The relationship between unemployment and fertility in Italy: A time-series analysis. Demographic Research, 34(1), 1–3.

Chelli, F. M., Ciommi, M., Emili, A., Gigliarano, C., and Taralli, S. (2016). Assessing the Equitable and Sustainable Well-Being of the Italian Provinces. International Journal of Uncertainty, Fuzziness and Knowlege-Based Systems, 24, 39–62.

Chelli, F., Gigliarano, C., and Mattioli, E. (2009). The impact of inflation on heterogeneous groups of households: An application to Italy. Economics Bulletin, 29(2), 1276–1295.

Cherlin, A., Cumberworth, E., Morgan, S. P., and Wimer, C. (2013). The effects of the Great Recession on family structure and fertility. The Annals of the American Academy of Political and Social Science, 650(1), 214–223.

Chi, G., and Zhu, J. (2008). Spatial regression models for demographic analysis. Population Research and Policy Review, 27(1), 17–42.

Chorianopoulos, I., Pagonis, T., Koukoulas, S., and Drymoniti, S. (2010). Planning, competitiveness and sprawl in the Mediterranean city: The case of Athens. Cities, 27(4), 249–259.

Chorianopoulos, I., Tsilimigkas, G., Koukoulas, S., and Balatsos, T. (2014). The shift to competitiveness and a new phase of sprawl in the Mediterranean city: Enterprises guiding growth in Messoghia–Athens. Cities, 39, 133–143.

Ciommi, M., Chelli, F. M., Carlucci, M., and Salvati, L. (2018). Urban growth and demographic dynamics in southern Europe: Toward a new statistical approach to regional science. Sustainability, 10(8), 2765.

Ciommi, M., Chelli, F. M., and Salvati, L. (2019). Integrating parametric and non-parametric multivariate analysis of urban growth and commuting patterns in a European metropolitan area. Quality and Quantity, 3(2), 957–979.

Ciommi, M., Egidi, G., Vardopoulos, I., Chelli, F. M., and Salvati, L. (2022). Toward a 'Migrant Trap'? Local Development, Urban Sustainability, Sociodemographic Inequalities, and the Economic Decline in a Mediterranean Metropolis. Social Sciences, 12(1), 26.

Ciommi, M., Gigliarano, C., Emili, A., Taralli, S., and Chelli, F. M. (2017). A new class of composite indicators for measuring well-being at the local level: An application to the Equitable and Sustainable Well-being (BES) of the Italian Provinces. Ecological Indicators, 76, 281–296.

Coccossis H., Economou D. and Petrakos G. (2005). The ESDP relevance to a distant partner: Greece. European Planning Studies, 13(2): 253–264.

Cohen, B. (2006). Urbanization in Developing Countries: Current Trends, Future Projections, and Key Challenges for Sustainability. Technology and Society, 28(1–2), 63–80.

Colantoni, A., Grigoriadis, E., Sateriano, A., Venanzoni, G., and Salvati, L. (2016) Cities as selective land predators? A lesson on urban growth, deregulated planning and sprawl containment. Science of the Total Environment, 545–546, 329–339.

Colantoni, A., Mavrakis, A., Sorgi, T., and Salvati, L. (2015). Towards a 'polycentric' landscape? Reconnecting fragments into an integrated network of coastal forests in Rome. Rendiconti Lincei, 26, 615–624.

Coleman, D. (2006). Immigration and ethnic change in low-fertility countries: A third demographic transition. Population and Development Review, 401–446.

Comer, D., and Greene, J. (2015). The development and application of a land-use diversity index for Oklahoma City, OK. Applied Geography, 60, 46–57.

Conti S. and Segre A. (1998). Mediterranean geographies. Geo – Italy 3. Società Geografica Italiana & CNR – Italian Committee for International Geographical Union, Rome.

Cortesi, A., Vardopoulos, I., and Salvati, L. (2022). A Partial Least Squares Analysis of the Perceived Impact of Sustainable Real Estate Design upon Wellbeing. Urban Science, 6(4), 69.

Couch, C., Petschel-Held, G., and Leontidou, L. (2007). Urban sprawl in Europe: landscapes, land-use change and policy. Oxford: Blackwell.

Cuadrado-Ciuraneta, S., Durà-Guimerà, A., and Salvati, L. (2017). Not only tourism: unravelling suburbanization, second-home expansion and "rural" sprawl in Catalonia, Spain. Urban Geography, 38(1), 66–89.

D'Agata, A., Ponza, D., Strolu, F. A., Vardopoulos, I., Rontos, K., Escrivà, F., Chelli, F., Alaimo, L. S., Luca, S., and Nickayin, S. S. (2023). Toward sustainable development trajectories? Estimating urban footprints from high-resolution copernicus layers in Athens, Greece. Land, 12(8), 1490.

Dahly, D. L., and Adair, L. S. (2007). Quantifying the urban environment: A scale measure of urbanicity outperforms the urban–rural dichotomy. Social Science & Medicine, 64(7), 1407–1419.

Dal Pozzolo L. (2002). Fuori città, senza campagna. Franco Angeli, Milano.

Davies, W. K., and Donoghue, D. P. (1993). Economic diversification and group stability in an urban system: the case of Canada, 1951–86. Urban Studies, 30(7), 1165–1186.

Davis, J. C., and Henderson, J. V. (2003). Evidence on the political economy of the urbanization process. Journal of Urban Economics, 53(1), 98–125.

Davoudi S. (2003). Polycentricity in European spatial planning: from an analytical tool to a normative agenda. European Planning Studies, 11(8): 979–999.

De Beer, J., and Deerenberg, I. (2007). An explanatory model for projecting regional fertility differences in the Netherlands. Population Research and Policy Review, 26, 511–528.

De Rosa, S., and Salvati, L. (2016). Beyond a 'side street story'? Naples from spontaneous centrality to entropic polycentricism, towards a 'crisis city'. Cities, 51, 74–83.

Deffontaines P. (1972). El Mediterraneo. La tierra, el mar, los hombres. Editorial Juventud, Barcellona.

Delladetsima P.M. (2006). The emerging property development pattern in Greece and its impact on spatial development. European Urban and Regional Studies, 13(3), 245–278.

Delladetsima, P. M. (2012). Sustainable Development and Spatial Planning: Some considerations arising from the Greek case. European Journal of Spatial Development, 46, 1–21.

Desrochers, P. (2001). Local Diversity, Human Creativity and Technological Innovation. Growth and Change, 32, 369–394.

Desrochers, P., and Hospers, G.J. (2007). Cities and the Economic Development of Nations: An Essay on Jane Jacobs' Contribution to Economic Theory. Canadian Journal of Regional Science, 30(1), 119–134.

Dewilde, C., and De Decker, P. (2016) Changing Inequalities in Housing Outcomes across Western Europe. Housing, Theory and Society, 33(2), 121–161.

Di Feliciantonio, C., and Salvati, L. (2015). 'Southern' Alternatives of Urban Diffusion: Investigating Settlement Characteristics and Socio-Economic Patterns in Three Mediterranean Regions. Tijdschrift Voor Economische En Sociale Geografie, 106(4), 453–470.

Dijkstra, L., Garcilazo, E., and McCann, P. (2015). The effects of the global financial crisis on European regions and cities. Journal of Economic Geography, 15(5), 935–949.

Domene, E., Sauri, D., and Parés, M. (2005). Urbanization and sustainable resource use: the case of garden watering in the metropolitan region of Barcelona. Urban Geography, 26(6), 520–535.

Domene, E., and Sauri, D. (2006). Urbanization and water consumption: influential factors in the metropolitan region of Barcelona. Urban Studies, 43(9), 1605–1623.

Dommelen, P. van, and Knapp, A. B. (Eds.). (2010). Material Connections in the Ancient Mediterranean. Routledge.

Doukas, Y. E. (2011). Economic activity and productivity: The role of density in the Greek urban space. European Association of Geographers Annual Meeting "Geography: Your World – A European Perspective", 2–5 June 2011. Athens, Greece.

Doukas, Y. E., Maravegias, N., and Andreou, G. (Eds.). (2022). Η χωρική διάσταση της ευρωπαϊκής ολοκλήρωσης: σύγκλιση ή απόκλιση; Dionicos: Athens, Greece. ISBN: 978-6185-6650-3-6.

Doukas, Y. E., Salvati, L., and Vardopoulos, I. (2023). Unraveling the European agricultural policy sustainable development trajectory. Land, 12(9), 1749.

Dura-Guimera, A. (2003). Population deconcentration and social restructuring in Barcelona, a European Mediterranean city. Cities, 20, 387–394.

Duranton, G., and Puga, D. (2000). Diversity and Specialisation in Cities: Why, Where and When Does it Matter? Urban Studies, 37, 533–555.

Duranton, G., and Puga, D. (2001). Nursery cities: Urban diversity, process innovation, and the life cycle of products. American Economic Review, 91(5), 1454–1477.

Duvernoy, I., Zambon, I., Sateriano, A., and Salvati, L. (2018). Pictures from the other side of the fringe: Urban growth and peri-urban agriculture in a post-industrial city (Toulouse, France). Journal of Rural Studies, 57, 25–35.

Economidou, E. (1993). The Attic landscape throughout the centuries and its human degradation. Landscape and Urban Planning, 24, 33–37.

Economou D. (1997). The planning system and rural land use control in Greece: an European perspective. European Planning Studies, 5(4), 461–476.

Edgington, D. W. (1982). Organisational and Technological Change and the Future Role of the Central Business District: an Australian Example. Urban Studies, 19(3), 281–292.

Ejermo, O. (2005). Technological diversity and Jacobs' externality hypothesis revisited. Growth and Change, 36(2), 167–195.

Ellerman, D. (2005). How Do We Grow? Jane Jacobs on Diversification and Specialization. Challenge, 48(3), 50–83.

Escolano, J. J., Pedreño, J. N., Lucas, I. G., Almendro Candel, M. B., and Zorpas, A. A. (2018). Decreased Organic Carbon Associated With Land Management in Mediterranean Environments. In M. Á. Muñoz and R. Zornoza (Eds.), Soil Management and Climate Change. Effects on Organic Carbon, Nitrogen Dynamics, and Greenhouse Gas Emissions, (pp. 1–13). Elsevier: Cambridge, MA, USA. ISBN: 978-0-12-812128-3.

European Environment Agency (2006). Urban Sprawl in Europe. The ignored challenge. European Environment Agency. Copenhagen, DK: Office for Official Publications of the European Communities.

European Environment Agency (2011). Mapping guide for a European urban atlas. EEA: Copenhagen (Version 1.1).

Evans, A., and Gray, E. (2018). Modelling Variation in Fertility Rates Using Geographically Weighted Regression. Spatial Demography, 6, 121–140.

Farinelli F. (1998). Il Mediterraneo, la differenza, il differimento. Geotema, 12, 57–62.

Fekade, W. (2000). Deficits of formal urban land management and informal responses under rapid urban growth, an international perspective. Habitat International, 24(2), 127–150.

Feleki, E., Achillas, C., Vlachokostas, C., Michailidou, A., Ortega, L., and Moussiopoulos, N. (2018). Preservation of the Mediterranean Identity: An Intra-City Analysis Towards a Macro-Regional Approach for the Characterisation of Urban Sustainability. Sustainability, 10(10), 3551.

Filandri, M., and Olagnero, M. (2014) Housing inequality and social class in Europe. Housing Studies, 29(7), 977–993.

Fincher, R., and Jacobs, J. M. (1998). Cities of difference. Guilford Press, New York.

Fiori, F., Graham, E., and Feng, Z. (2014). Geographical variations in fertility and transition to second and third birth in Britain. Advances in Life Course Research, 21, 149–167.

Fischer, C. S., Stockmayer, G., Stiles, J., and Hout, M. (2004). Distinguishing the geographic levels and social dimensions of US metropolitan segregation, 1960–2000. Demography, 41(1), 37–59.

Frejka, T., and Sobotka, T. (2008). Fertility in Europe: Diverse, delayed and below replacement. Demographic Research, 19, 15–46.

Frenken, K., Van Oort, F., and Verburg, T. (2007). Related variety, unrelated variety and regional economic growth, Regional Studies, 41, 685–697.

Gabriel S. A., and Rosenthal S. S. (2015). The boom, the bust and the future of homeownership. Real Estate Economics, 43(2), 334–374.

Galster, G., Hanson, R., Ratcliffe, M. R., Wolman, H., Coleman, S., and Freihage, J. (2001). Wrestling sprawl to the ground: defining and measuring an elusive concept. Housing Policy Debate, 12(4), 681–717.

Garcia, M. (2010). The breakdown of the Spanish urban growth model: Social and territorial effects of the global crisis. International Journal of Urban and Regional Research, 34(4), 967–980.

Gavalas, V. S., Rontos, K., and Salvati, L. (2014). Who becomes an unwed mother in Greece? Socio-demographic and geographical aspects of an emerging phenomenon. Population, Space, and Place, 20(3), 250–263.

Georgiadis, K. (2011). Fertile debates: a comparative account of low fertility in the British and Greek national press. European Journal of Population, 27(2), 243–262.

Giannakourou, G. (2005). Transforming spatial planning policy in Mediterranean countries. Europeanization and domestic change. European Planning Studies, 13(2), 253–264.

Gigliarano, C., and Chelli, F. M. (2016). Measuring inter-temporal intragenerational mobility: an application to the Italian labour market. Quality and Quantity, 50(1), 89–102.

Gil-Alonso, F., Bayona-i-Carrasco, J., and Pujadas-i-Rúbies, I. (2016). From boom to crash: Spanish urban areas in a decade of change (2001–2011). European Urban and Regional Studies, 23(2), 198–216.

Gilli, F. (2009). Sprawl or reagglomeration? The dynamics of employment deconcentration and industrial transformation in greater Paris. Urban Studies, 46(7), 1385–1420.

Gkartzios, M. (2013). 'Leaving Athens': Narratives of counterurbanisation in times of crisis. Journal of Rural Studies, 32, 158–167.

Gkartzios, M., and Scott, K. (2015). A cultural panic in the province? Counterurban mobilities, creativity, and crisis in Greece. Population, Space and Place, 21(8), 843–855.

Grant, J. (2002). Mixed Use in Theory and Practice: Canadian Experience with Implementing a Planning Principle. Journal of the American Planning Association, 68(1), 71–84.

Grant, J., and Perrott, K. (2009). Producing diversity in a new urbanism community: Policy and practice. Town Planning Review, 80(3), 267–289.

Grekousis, G., Manetos, P., and Photis, Y. N. (2013). Modeling urban evolution using neural networks, fuzzy logic and GIS: The case of the Athens metropolitan area. Cities, 30, 193–203.

Haase, A., Kabisch, S., Steinführer, A., Bouzarovski, S., Hall, R., and Ogden, P. (2010). Spaces of reurbanisation: exploring the demographic dimension of inner-city residential change in a European setting. Population, Space and Place, 16(5), 443–463.

Hahs, A. K., and McDonnell, M. J. (2006). Selecting independent measures to quantify Melbourne's urban–rural gradient. Landscape and Urban Planning, 78(4), 435–448.

Halbac-Cotoara-Zamfir, R., Marucci, A., Salvia, R., Quaranta, G., Sateriano, A., Cecchini, M., and Bianchini, L. (2022). Caring of the Fringe? Mediterranean Desertification between Peri-Urban Ecology and Socioeconomics. Sustainability, 14(3), 1426.

Hall, P., and Pain, K. (2006). The polycentric metropolis. Learning from mega-city regions in Europe. London, UK: Earthscan.

Hank, K. (2002). Regional social contexts and individual fertility decisions: A multilevel analysis of first and second births in Western Germany. European Journal of Population, 18(3), 281–299.

Hanson, G. H. (2001). Scale economies and the geographic concentration of industry. Journal of Economic Geography, 1(3), 255–276.

Herrschel, T. (2009). City regions, polycentricity and the construction of peripheralities through governance. Urban Research and Practice, 2(3), 240–250.

Hill, D. R. (1988). Jane Jacobs' ideas on big, diverse cities: A review and commentary. Journal of the American Planning Association, 54(3), 302–314.

Hirt, S. (2012). Mixed use by default: how the Europeans (don't) zone. Journal of Planning Literature, 27(4), 375–393.

Hirt, S. (2016). Rooting out mixed use: Revisiting the original rationales. Land Use Policy, 50, 134–147.

Hoyler, M., Kloosterman, R. C., and Sokol, M. (2008). Polycentric puzzles: emerging megacity regions seen through the lens of advanced producer services. Regional Studies, 42, 1055–1064.

Iceland, J. (2004). Beyond Black and White Metropolitan residential segregation in multi-ethnic America. Social Science Research, 33, 248–271.

Inostroza, L. (2014). Measuring urban ecosystem functions through 'Technomass' - A novel indicator to assess urban metabolism. Ecological Indicators, 42, 10–19.

Johnson, M. P. (2001). Environmental impacts of urban sprawl: a survey of the literature and proposed research agenda. Environment and Planning A, 33(4), 717–735.

Kabisch, N., and Haase, D. (2011). Diversifying European agglomerations: evidence of urban population trends for the 21st century. Population, Space and Place, 17(3), 236–253.

Kahn, M. (2000). The Environmental Impact of Suburbanization. Journal of Policy Analysis and Management, 19(4), 569–586.

Kaika, M. (2003). Constructing Scarcity and Sensationalising Water Politics: 170 Days That Shook Athens. Antipode, 35(5), 919–954.

Kaika, M. (2012). The economic crisis seen from the everyday. City, 16(4), 422–430.

Kallis, G. (2010). Coevolution in water resource development. The vicious cycle of water supply and demand in Athens, Greece. Ecological Economics, 69(4), 796–809.

Karavitis, C. (1998). Drought and urban water supply: the case of metropolitan Athens. Water Policy, 1(5), 505–524.

Karytsas, S., Vardopoulos, I., and Theodoropoulou, E. (2019). Factors affecting residents' attitude toward sustainable tourism development. Tourismos, 14(1), 1–40.

Kasanko, M., Barredo, J. I., Lavalle, C., McCormick, N., Demicheli, L., Sagris, V., and Brezger, A. (2006). Are European Cities Becoming Dispersed? A Comparative Analysis of Fifteen European Urban Areas. Landscape and Urban Planning, 77, 111–130.

Kayser, B. (1996). Il Mediterraneo. Geografia della frattura. Jaca Book, Milano.

Kazemzadeh-Zow, A., Zanganeh Shahraki, S., Salvati, L., and Samani, N. N. (2017). A spatial zoning approach to calibrate and validate urban growth models. International Journal of Geographical Information Science, 31(4), 763–782.

Kazepov, Y. (2005). Cities of Europe: Changing Contexts, Local Arrangements, and the Challenge to Urban Cohesion. Oxford, UK: Blackwell.

Kempton, Y., Salvati, L., and Vardopoulos, I. (2022). Long-term planning and development for urban and regional inclusion, safety, resilience, and sustainability. Insights from Singapore. Region & Periphery, 14(10), 58–78.

Kleinhans, R. (2004). Social implications of housing diversification in urban renewal: A review of recent literature. Journal of Housing and the Built Environment, 19(4), 367–390.

Kloosterman, R. C., and Musterd, S. (2001). The polycentric urban region: towards a research agenda. Urban Studies, 38, 623–633.

Knieling, J. (2015). Cities in Crisis: Socio-spatial Impacts of the Economic Crisis in Southern European Cities. London: Routledge.

Kohler, H. P., Billari, F. C., and Ortega, J. A. (2002). The emergence of lowest-low fertility in Europe during the 1990s. Population and Development Review, 28(4), 641–680.

Konchak, W., and Pascual, U. (2006). Converging economic paradigms for a constructive environmental policy discourse. Environmental Science & Policy, 9(1), 10–21.

Kourliouros, E. (1997). Planning industrial location in Greater Athens: the interaction between deindustrialization and anti-industrialism during the 1980s. European Planning Studies, 5(4), 435–460.

Kroll, F., and Kabisch, N. (2012). The Relation of Diverging Urban Growth Processes and Demographic Change along an Urban–Rural Gradient. Population, Space and Place, 18(3), 260–276.

Kulu, H. (2013). Why do fertility levels vary between urban and rural areas? Regional Studies, 47(6), 895–912.

Kulu, H., and Boyle, P. J. (2009). High fertility in city suburbs: Compositional or contextual effects? European Journal of Population, 25(2), 157–174.

Kulu, H., Boyle, P. J., and Anderson, G. (2009). High Suburban fertility: Evidence from Four Northern European Countries. Demographic Research, 31, 915–944.

Kulu, H., and Vikat, A. (2007). Fertility differences by housing type: The effect of housing conditions or of selective moves? Demographic Research, 17(26), 775–802.

Lagarias, A., and Sayas, J. (2018). Urban sprawl in the Mediterranean: Evidence from coastal medium-sized cities. Regional Science Inquiry, 10(3), 15–32.

Lamonica, G. R., and Chelli, F. M. (2018). The performance of non-survey techniques for constructing sub-territorial input-output tables. Papers in Regional Science, 97(4), 1169–1202.

Lauf, S., Haase, D., Seppelt, R., and Schwarz, N. (2012). Simulating demography and housing demand in an urban region under scenarios of growth and shrinkage. Environment and Planning B: Planning and Design, 39(2), 229–246.

Lee, K. O., and Painter, G. (2013). What happens to household formation in a recession? Journal of Urban Economics, 76, 93–109.

Lemonakis, C., Alexopoulos, G., Garefalakis, A., and Garefalakis, S. (2024). Trends and new elements in urban hierarchy research: the Greek paradigm. The Annals of Regional Science, 72, 335–354.

Leontidou, L. (1990). The Mediterranean city in transition. Cambridge University Press, Cambridge.

Leontidou, L. (1993). Postmodernism and the City: Mediterranean versions. Urban Studies, 30, 949–965.

Leontidou, L. (1996). Alternatives to modernism in (Southern) urban theory: Exploring in-between spaces. International Journal of Urban and Regional Research, 20(2), 180–197.

Leontidou, L. (2014). The crisis and its discourses: Quasi-Orientalist attacks on Mediterranean urban spontaneity, informality and joie de vivre. City, 18(4–5), 551–562.

Lerch, M. (2019). Regional variations in the rural-urban fertility gradients in global South. PloS One, 14(7), 1–19.

Lesthaeghe, R., and Lopez-Gay, A. (2013). Spatial continuities and discontinuities in two successive demographic transitions: Spain and Belgium, 1880–2010. Demographic Research, 28, 77–136.

Leto, S. M., and Hadjibiros, K. (2012). The growing water imprint of Athens (Greece) throughout history. Regional Environmental Change, 12, 337–345.

Liu, L. (2005). Fertility trends in China's more developed urban districts: The case of four cities. Population, Space and Place, 11(5), 411–424.

Longhi, C., and Musolesi, A. (2007). European cities in the process of economic integration: towards structural convergence. Annals of Regional Science, 41, 333–351.

Ludlow, P. (1994). Europe and the Mediterrranean. Brassey's, London.

Malheiros, J. (2002). Ethni-cities: residential patterns in the northern European and mediterranean metropolises- implications for policy design. International Journal of Population Geography, 8(2), 107–134.

Maloutas, T., and Karadimitriou, N. (2001). Vertical social differentiation in Athens: alternative or complement to community segregation. International Journal of Urban and Regional Research, 25(4), 699–716.

Maloutas, T. (1993). Social segregation in Athens. Antipode, 25(3), 223–239.

Maloutas, T. (2004). Segregation and residential mobility. Socially entrapped social mobility and its impact on segregation in Athens. European Urban and Regional Studies, 11(2), 171–87.
Maloutas, T. (2007). Socio-economic classification models and contextual difference: The "European socio-economic classes" (ESeC) from a South European angle. South European Society & Politics, 12(4), 443–460.
Manola, M. (2022). Contribution of the Venetian Monuments of Rhodes to Cultural Tourism and the Local Development of the Island. Open Journal for Research in Economics, 5(1), 35–42.
Maravegias, N., and Doukas, Y. E. (2012). A stategy for rural development in Greece: The case of Island Areas. Region & Periphery, 1, 37–56.
Markusen, A., and Schrock, G. (2006). The distinctive city: divergent patterns in growth, hierarchy and specialisation. Urban Studies, 43(8), 1301–1323.
Martín García, T. (2010). The impact of occupational sex-composition on women's fertility in Spain. European Societies, 12(1), 113–133.
Massey, D. S., and Denton, N. A. (1988). The Dimensions of Residential Segregation. Social Forces, 67(2), 281–315.
Matvejevic, P. (1996). Mediterraneo. Un nuovo breviario. Garzanti, Milano.
Matvejevic, P. (1998). Il Mediterraneo e l'Europa. Garzanti, Milano.
Meijers, E., and Burger, M. (2010). Spatial structure and productivity in US metropolitan areas. Environment and Planning A, 42, 1383–1402.
Meléndez-Pastor, I., Pedreño, J. N., Lucas, I. G., and Zorpas, A. A. (2017). A Model for Evaluating Soil Vulnerability to Erosion Using Remote Sensing Data and A Fuzzy Logic System. In Modern Fuzzy Control Systems and Its Applications. London, UK. InTech.
Michielin, F. (2004). Lowest low fertility in an urban context: The role of migration in Turin, Italy. Population, Space and Place, 10(4), 331–347.
Minca, C. (2003). Critical peripheries. Environment and Planning D: Society and Space, 21, 160–168.
Minca, C. (2004). Orizzonte mediterraneo. Cedam, Padova.
Munafò, M., Salvati, L., and Zitti, M. (2013). Estimating soil sealing rate at national level - Italy as a case study. Ecological Indicators, 26, 137–140.
Muniz, J. O. (2009). Spatial dependence and heterogeneity in ten years of fertility decline in Brazil. Population Review, 48(2), 32–65.
Muñoz, F. (2003). Lock living: Urban sprawl in Mediterranean cities. Cities, 20(6), 381–385.
Muscarà, C. (1986). Megalopoli mediterranea. Franco Angeli, Milano.

Musterd, S., and Ostendorf, W. (1998). Urban segregation and the welfare state: Inequality and exclusion in western cities. London, UK: Routledge.

O'Donoghue, D. (1999). The relationship between diversification and growth: some evidence from the British urban system 1978 to 1991. International Journal of Urban and Regional Research, 23(3), 549–566.

O'Donoghue, D., and Townshend, I. J. (2005). Diversification, specialization, convergence and divergence of sectoral employment structures in the British urban system, 1991–2001. Regional Studies, 39, 585–601.

Ogden, P. E., and Hall, R. (2000). Households, reurbanisation and the rise of living alone in the principal French cities 1975–1990. Urban Studies, 37(2), 367–390.

Ottaviano, G. I., and Peri, G. (2006). The economic value of cultural diversity: evidence from US cities. Journal of Economic Geography, 6(1), 9–44.

Oueslati, W., Alvanides, S., and Garrod, G. (2015). Determinants of urban sprawl in European cities. Urban Studies, 52(9), 1594–1614.

Pacione, M. (2003). Urban environmental quality and human wellbeing – a social geographical perspective. Landscape and Urban Planning, 65(1–2), 19–30.

Page, M., Parisel, C., Pumain, D., and Sanders, L. (2001). Knowledge-based simulation of settlement systems. Computers, Environment and Urban Systems, 25(2), 167–193.

Panagiotopoulos, P. (2023). Βιώσιμη Περιφερειακή Ανάπτυξη. Αθλητισμός-Τουρισμός. Athens, Greece: Nomiki Bibliothiki. ISBN: 9786180801446

Panori, A., Psycharis, Y., and Ballas, D. (2019). Spatial segregation and migration in the city of Athens: Investigating the evolution of urban socio-spatial immigrant structures. Population Space and Place, 25(5), e2209.

Papamichael, I., Voukkali, I., and Zorpas, A. A. (2022). Mediterranean: main environmental issues and concerns. Euro-Mediterranean Journal for Environmental Integration, 7(4), 477–481.

Parr, J. B. (2004). The polycentric urban region: a closer inspection. Regional Studies, 38, 231–240.

Parr, J. B. (2008). Cities and regions: problems and potentials. Environment and Planning A, 40, 3009–3026.

Passas, I., Ragazou, K., Zafeiriou, E., Garefalakis, A., and Zopounidis, C. (2022). ESG Controversies: A Quantitative and Qualitative Analysis for the Sociopolitical Determinants in EU Firms. Sustainability, 14(19), 12879.

Pérez, J. M. G. (2010). The real estate and economic crisis: An opportunity for urban return and rehabilitation policies in Spain. Sustainability, 2(6), 1571–1601.

Pili, S., Grigoriadis, E., Carlucci, M., Clemente, M., and Salvati, L. (2017). Towards sustainable growth? A multi-criteria assessment of (changing) urban forms. Ecological Indicators, 76, 71–80.

Pison, G. (2011). Two children per woman in France in 2010: Is French fertility immune to economic crisis? Population & Societies, 476, 1–4.

Potter, J. E., Schmertmann, C. P., Assunção, R. M., and Cavenaghi, S. M. (2010). Mapping the timing, pace, and scale of the fertility transition in Brazil. Population and Development Review, 36(2), 283–307.

Qureshi, S., Haase, D., and Coles, R. (2014). The Theorized Urban Gradient (TUG) method - A conceptual framework for socioecological sampling in complex urban agglomerations. Ecological Indicators, 36, 100–110.

Reeder, D., and Rodger, R. (2001). Industrialisation and the city economy. In The Cambridge Urban History of Britain, (pp. 551–592). Cambridge University Press.

Rees, P., Bell, M., Kupiszewski, M., Kupiszewska, D., Ueffing, P., Bernard, A., Edwards, E. C., and Stillwell, J. (2017). The impact of internal migration on population redistribution: An international comparison. Population, Space and Place, 23(6), e2036.

Rees, P., Wohland, P., and Norman, P. (2013). The demographic drivers of future ethnic group populations for UK local areas 2001–2051. The Geographical Journal, 179(1), 44–60.

Remoundou, K., Gkartzios, M., and Garrod, G. (2016). Conceptualizing Mobility in Times of Crisis: Towards Crisis-Led Counterurbanization? Regional Studies, 50(10), 1663–1674.

Ribeiro, O. (1972). Il Mediterraneo. Ambiente e tradizione. Mursia, Milano.

Robinson, J. (2002). Global and world cities: a view from off the map. International Journal of Urban and Regional Research, 26(3), 531–554.

Rodriguez-Rodriguez, V. (2000). The seven demographic Spains. Intermunicipal contrasts in age structure: fertility and migration are the determining factors. Espace, Populations, Sociétés, 18(3), 425–435.

Rontos, K. (2007). Prospects for a new family formation and for its impact on fertility: some research evidences from Greece. Statistical Review, 3(1), 1–9.

Rontos, K. (2010). Demographic trends, young people's attitudes towards marriage and socio-economic changes related to family formation in Greece and in selected European Countries: A comparative analysis based on official and survey research data. International Journal of Criminology and Sociological Theory, 3(2), 543–562.

Rontos, K., Grigoriadis, E., Sateriano, A., Syrmali, M., Vavouras, I., and Salvati, L. (2016). Lost in protest, found in segregation: Divided cities

in the light of the 2015 "Oχι" referendum in Greece. City, Culture and Society, 7(3), 139–148.
Rosenthal, S. S., and Strange, W. C. (2001). The determinants of agglomeration. Journal of Urban Economics, 50(2), 191–229.
Sabater, A., and Graham, E. (2019). International migration and fertility variation in Spain during the economic recession: A spatial Durbin approach. Applied Spatial Analysis and Policy, 12(3), 515–546.
Salvati, L. (2013). Monitoring high-quality soil consumption driven by urban pressure in a growing city (Rome, Italy). Cities, 31, 349–356.
Salvati, L. (2014). Agro-forest landscape and the 'fringe' city: A multivariate assessment of land-use changes in a sprawling region and implications for planning. Science of the Total Environment, 490, 715–723.
Salvati, L. (2016). The dark side of the crisis: disparities in per-capita income (2000–2012) and the urban-rural gradient in Greece. Tijdschrift voor Economische en Sociale Geografie, 107(5), 628–641.
Salvati, L. (2019). Examining urban functions along a metropolitan gradient: a geographically weighted regression tells you more. Letters in Spatial and Resource Sciences, 12(1), 19–40.
Salvati, L., and Morelli, V. G. (2014). Unveiling Urban Sprawl in the Mediterranean Region: Towards a Latent Urban Transformation? International Journal of Urban and Regional Research, 38(6), 1935–1953.
Salvati, L., and Vardopoulos, I. (2024). Intricacies of Mediterranean urban and regional dynamics. Euro-Mediterranean Journal for Environmental Integration, in press.
Salvati, L., Benassi, F., Miccoli, S., Rabiei-Dastjerdi, H., and Matthews, S. A. (2020). Spatial variability of total fertility rate and crude birth rate in a low-fertility country: patterns and trends in regional and local scale heterogeneity across Italy, 2002–2018. Applied Geography, 124, 102321.
Salvati, L., and Carlucci, M. (2011). The economic and environmental performances of rural districts in Italy: Are competitiveness and sustainability compatible targets? Ecological Economics, 70(12), 2446–2453.
Salvati, L., Ferrara, A., and Chelli, F. (2018). Long-term growth and metropolitan spatial structures: an analysis of factors influencing urban patch size under different economic cycles. Geografisk Tidsskrift-Danish Journal of Geography, 118(1), 56–71.
Salvati, L., Gargiulo Morelli, V., Rontos, K., and Sabbi, A. (2013). Latent Exurban Development: City Expansion along the Rural-To-Urban Gradient in Growing and Declining Regions of Southern Europe. Urban Geography, 34(3), 376–394.

Salvati, L., Sateriano, A., Saradakou, E., and Grigoriadis, E. (2016). 'Land-use mixité': Evaluating urban hierarchy and the urban-to-rural gradient with an evenness-based approach. Ecological Indicators, 70, 35–42.

Salvatori, F. (ed.) (2008). Il Mediterraneo delle città. Scambi, confronti, culture, rappresentazioni. Viella, Roma.

Salvia, R., Quaranta, V., Sateriano, A., and Quaranta, G. (2022). Land Resource Depletion, Regional Disparities, and the Claim for a Renewed 'Sustainability Thinking' under Early Desertification Conditions. Resources, 11(3), 28.

Sassen, S. (2010). The city: its return as a lens for social theory. City, Culture and Society, 1(1), 3–11.

Sauri, D. (2003). Lights and shadows of urban water demand management. The case of the metropolitan region of Barcelona. European Planning Studies, 11(3), 229–243.

Schmidt, C. G. (1977). Influence of land-use diversity upon neighborhood success: An analysis of Jacobs' theory. Annals of Regional Science, 11(1), 53–65.

Schneider, D. (2015). The Great Recession, fertility, and uncertainty: evidence from the United States. Journal of Marriage and Family, 77, 1144–1156.

Schneider, F., Kallis, G., and Martinez-Alier, J. (2010). Crisis or opportunity? Economic degrowth for social equity and ecological sustainability. Introduction to this special issue. Journal of Cleaner Production, 18(6), 511–518.

Scott, A. J. (2001). Global city-regions. Trends, theory, policy. Oxford University Press, Oxford.

Seltzer, N. (2019). Beyond the Great Recession: labor market polarization and ongoing fertility decline in the United States. Demography, 56(4), 1463–1493.

Serra, P., Vera, A., Tulla, A. F., and Salvati, L. (2014). Beyond urban–rural dichotomy: exploring socioeconomic and land-use processes of change in Spain (1991–2011). Applied Geography, 55, 71–81.

Smets, P., and Salman, T. (2008). Countering urban segregation: Theoretical and policy innovations from around the globe. Urban Studies, 45(7), 1307–1332.

Souliotis, N. (2013). Cultural economy, sovereign debt crisis and the importance of local contexts: The case of Athens. Cities, 33, 61–68.

Šprocha, B., and Bleha, B. (2018). Does Socio-Spatial Segregation Matter? 'Islands' of High Romany Fertility in Slovakia. Tijdschrift voor economische en sociale geografie, 109(2), 239–255.

Stanley, B. (2012). An historical perspective on the viability of urban diversity: lessons from socio-spatial identity construction in nineteenth-century Algiers and Cape Town. Journal of Urbanism: International Research on Placemaking and Urban Sustainability, 5(1), 67–86.

Stockdale, A. (2016). Contemporary and 'Messy' Rural In-migration Processes: Comparing Counterurban and Lateral Rural Migration. Population, Space and Place, 22(6), 599–616.

Stott, M. A., Kenny, M., and Kertzer, D. E. (1984). Urban Life in Mediterranean Europe: Anthropological Perspectives. Man, 19(4), 690.

Swyngedouw, E. (2004). Social power and the urbanization of water. Oxford, UK: Oxford University Press.

Talen, E. (2005). Land-use zoning and human diversity: Exploring the connection. Journal of Urban Planning and Development, 131(4), 214–232.

Talen, E. (2006). Design that enables diversity: The complications of a planning ideal. Journal of Planning Literature, 20(3), 233–249.

Theodora, Y. (2020). Cultural Heritage as a Means for Local Development in Mediterranean Historic Cities—The Need for an Urban Policy. Heritage, 3(2), 152–175.

Thygesen, L. C., Knudsen, L. B., and Keiding, N. (2005). Modelling regional variation of first-time births in Denmark 1980–1994 by an age-period-cohort model. Demographic Research, 13(23), 573–590.

Tochterman, B. (2012). Theorizing neoliberal urban development: A genealogy from Richard Florida to Jane Jacobs. Radical History Review, 112, 65–87.

Torisu, E. (2007). Policies to Enhance City Attractiveness: Achievements and New Challenges, (pp. 339–351).

Torrens, P. M. (2008). A toolkit for measuring sprawl. Applied Spatial Analysis and Policy, 1, 5–36.

Tragaki, A., and Bagavos, C. (2019). Fertility variations in the recession context: the case of Greece. Genus, 75(1), 18.

Troin, J.F. (1997). Le metropoli del mediterraneo. Città di frontiera, città cerniera, Milano, Jaca Book.

Tsilika, E. (2017). The Creation of Civic Identity in Post-war Corporate Architecture: Marcel Breuer's Bijenkorf in Rotterdam (1953–57). In J. Gossey and T. Avermaete (Eds.), Shopping Towns Europe. Commercial Collectivity and the Architecture of the Shopping Centre, 1945–1975. pp. 183–195. London, UK.

Tsilika, E. (2021). "Sun and Shadow": Exploring Marcel Breuer's Basic Design Principle. Architecture and Culture, 9(2), 332–360.

Tsoulouvis, L. (1996). Urban planning, social policy and new forms of social exclusion in Greek cities. International Journal of Urban and Regional Research, 20(4), 718–732.

Tumpel-Gugerell, G. and Mooslechner, P. (2003). Economic convergence and divergence in Europe. Growth and regional development in an enlarged European union. Chichester: Edward Elgar.

Turok, I., and Bailey, N. (2004). The theory of polynuclear urban regions and its application to central Scotland. European Planning Studies, 12(3), 371–389.

Vaiou, D. (1997). Facets of spatial development and planning in Greece. European Planning Studies, 5(4), 431–433.

Vaiou, D. (2004). The contested and negotiated dominance of Anglophone geography in Greece. Geoforum, 35, 529–531.

Van Criekingen, M. (2010). Gentrifying the re-urbanisation debate, not vice versa: the uneven socio-spatial implications of changing transitions to adulthood in Brussels. Population, Space and Place, 16(5), 381–394.

Van Oort, F., de Geus, S., and Dogaru, T. (2015). Related variety and regional economic growth in a cross-section of European urban regions. European Planning Studies, 23(6), 1110–1127.

Vandermotten, C., Halbert, L., Roelandts, M., and Cornut, P. (2008). European planning and the polycentric consensus: wishful thinking? Regional Studies, 42(8), 1205–1217.

Vardopoulos, I. (2019). Critical sustainable development factors in the adaptive reuse of urban industrial buildings. A fuzzy DEMATEL approach. Sustainable Cities and Society, 50, 101684.

Vardopoulos, I. (2022). Industrial building adaptive reuse for museum. Factors affecting visitors' perceptions of the sustainable urban development potential. Building and Environment, 222, 109391.

Vardopoulos, I., and Konstantinou, Z. (2017). Study of the possible links between CO_2 emissions and employment status. Sustainable Development, Culture, Traditions Journal, 1(B), 100–112.

Vardopoulos, I., Falireas, S., Konstantopoulos, I., Kaliora, E., and Theodoropoulou, E. (2018). Sustainability assessment of the agri-environmental practices in Greece. Indicators' comparative study. International Journal of Agricultural Resources, Governance and Ecology, 14(4), 368–399.

Vardopoulos, I., Giannopoulos, K., Papaefthymiou, E., Temponera, E., Chatzithanasis, G., Goussia-Rizou, M., Karymbalis, E., Michalakelis, C., Tsartas, P., and Sdrali, D. (2023). Urban buildings sustainable adaptive reuse into tourism accommodation establishments: a SOAR analysis. Discover Sustainability, 4(1), 50.

Vardopoulos, I., Ioannides, S., Georgiou, M., Voukkali, I., Salvati, L., and Doukas, Y. E. (2023). Shaping sustainable cities: A long-rerm GIS-emanated spatial analysis of settlement growth and planning in a coastal Mediterranean European city. Sustainability, 15(14), 11202.

Vardopoulos, I., Papoui-Evangelou, M., Nosovo, B., and Salvati, L. (2023). Smart 'tourist cities' revisited: Culture-led urban sustainability and the global real estate market. Sustainability, 15(5), 4313.

Vardopoulos, I., Tsilika, E., Sarantakou, E., Zorpas, A. A., Salvati, L., and Tsartas, P. (2021). An integrated SWOT-PESTLE-AHP model assessing sustainability in adaptive reuse projects. Applied Sciences, 11(15), 7134.

Vasanen, A. (2012). Functional polycentricity: examining metropolitan spatial structure through the connectivity of urban sub-centres. Urban Studies, 49(16), 3627–3644.

Venerandi, A., Zanella, M., Romice, O., Dibble, J., and Porta, S. (2017). Form and urban change–An urban morphometric study of five gentrified neighbourhoods in London. Environment and Planning B: Urban Analytics and City Science, 44(6), 1056–1076.

Vicino T.J., Hanlon B., and Rennie Short J. (2007). Megalopolis 50 Years on: the transformation of a city region. International Journal of Urban and Regional Research, 31(2), 344–367.

Vidal, M., Domene, E., and Sauri, D. (2011). Changing geographies of water-related consumption: residential swimming pools in suburban Barcelona. Area, 43(1), 67–75.

Viladecans-Marsal, E. (2004). Agglomeration economies and industrial location: city-level evidence. Journal of Economic Geography, 4(5), 565–582.

Vinci, S., Vardopoulos, I., and Salvati, L. (2023). A tale of a shrinking City? Exploring the complex interplay of socio-demographic dynamics in the recent development of Attica, Greece. Cities, 132, 104089.

Vitali, A., and Billari, F. C. (2017). Changing determinants of low fertility and diffusion: A spatial analysis for Italy. Population, Space and Place, 23(2), e1998.

Voss, P. R. (2007). Demography as a spatial social science. Population Research and Policy Review, 26(5), 457–476.

Vradis, A. (2014). Crisis-scapes suspended: Introduction. City, 18(4–5), 498–501.

Wachter, K. W. (2005). Spatial demography. Proceedings of the National Academy of Sciences, 102(43), 15299–15300.

Waldorf, B., and Franklin, R. (2002). Spatial dimensions of the Easterlin hypothesis: fertility variations in Italy. Journal of Regional Science, 42, 549–578.

Walford, N., and Kurek, S. (2016). Outworking of the Second Demographic Transition: National Trends and Regional Patterns of Fertility Change in Poland, and England and Wales, 2002–2012. Population, Space and Place, 22(6), 508–525.

Wang, D., and Chi, G. (2017). Different Places, Different Stories: A Study of Spatial Heterogeneity of County-Level Fertility in China. Demographic Research, 37, 493.

Ward, K., and Jonas, A. E. G. (2004). Competitive City-Regionalism as a Politics of Space: A Critical Reinterpretation of the New Regionalism. Environment and Planning A: Economy and Space, 36(12), 2119–2139.

Weeks, J. R., Getis, A., Hill, A. G., Gadalla, M. S., and Rashed, T. (2004). The fertility transition in Egypt: Intraurban patterns in Cairo. Annals of the Association of American Geographers, 94(1), 74–93.

Wessel, T., Turner, L. M., and Nordvik, V. (2018). Population dynamics and ethnic geographies in Oslo: the impact of migration and natural demographic change on ethnic composition and segregation. Journal of Housing and the Built Environment, 33(4), 789–805.

Wilson, B., and Kuha, J. (2018). Residential segregation and the fertility of immigrants and their descendants. Population, Space and Place, 24(3), e2098.

Wood, M. (2003). A balancing act? Tenure diversification in Australia and the UK. Urban Policy and Research, 21(1), 45–56.

Wood, S., and Dovey, K. (2015). Creative Multiplicities: Urban Morphologies of Creative Clustering. Journal of Urban Design, 20(1), 52–74.

Xanthos, G., Zopounidis, C., Garefalakis, A., Lemonakis, C., and Passas, I. (2022). Distinguish regional performance with the use of shift-share analysis and MCDA methods: a gross value added perspective. Operational Research, 22(2), 1363–1376.

Yang, R., and Jargowsky, P. A. (2006). Suburban development and economic segregation in the 1990s Journal of Urban Affairs, 28(3), 253–273.

Youn, H., Bettencourt, L. M., Lobo, J., Strumsky, D., Samaniego, H., and West, G. B. (2016). Scaling and universality in urban economic diversification. Journal of the Royal Society Interface, 13(114), 20150937.

Yüceşahin, M. M., and Özgür, E. M. (2008). Regional fertility differences in Turkey: persistent high fertility in the southeast. Population, Space and Place, 14(2), 135–158.

Zaidi, B., and Morgan, P. (2017). The second demographic transition theory: A Review and Appraisal. Annual Review of Sociology, 43, 473–492.

Zambon, I., Benedetti, A., Ferrara, C., and Salvati, L. (2018). Soil Matters? A Multivariate Analysis of Socioeconomic Constraints to Urban Expansion in Mediterranean Europe. Ecological Economics, 146, 173–183.

Zambon, I., Serra, P., Grigoriadis, E., Carlucci, M., and Salvati, L. (2017). Emerging urban centrality: An entropy-based indicator of polycentric development and economic growth. Land Use Policy, 68, 365–371.

Zuindeau, B. (2007). Territorial equity and sustainable development. Environmental Values, 16, 253–268.

3

The Extrinsic Manifestation of Sprawl: Complex Dynamics of Urbanization, Land Imperviousness, and Sustainability in Mediterranean Landscapes

Francisco Escrivà Saneugenio, Adele Sateriano, Luca Salvati, and Ioannis Vardopoulos

Soil sealing, the gradual depletion of natural resources through the extensive covering of land for constructions such as buildings and roads, is a global concern (Munafò *et al.*, 2013; Scalenghe and Marsan, 2009). Imperviousness, which signifies the irreversible alteration of a soil's permeable layer, serves as a crucial measure of soil consumption in both advanced and emerging economies (Bradec, 2009; Salvati and Lamonica, 2020). Recognizing soil as sealed is essential for assessing the impact of human activities, including the expansion of built-up areas and changes in runoff patterns due to construction (Wessolek, 2008). As a pivotal environmental indicator (see Inglezakis and Zorpas, 2014), land imperviousness rates aid in estimating human impacts and delineating the extent of built-up areas (Salvati, 2014). This information is vital for understanding alterations in runoff patterns resulting from construction activities (Miller *et al.*, 2015; Lee and Heaney, 2003). In fragile ecosystems, the increase in land imperviousness accelerates landscape degradation and heightens vulnerability to climate change, soil erosion, wildfires, and water scarcity (Johnson 2001, Byrne *et al.* 2007, Poelmans *et al.* 2010; Vardopoulos and Karytsas, 2019). The extent of soil sealing all around the world is so intense that it deserves specific monitoring actions, as documented in Figure 3.1. The continuous monitoring of impervious land across various spatial scales emerges as a crucial tool for assessing natural resources and shaping urban containment strategies (Weber *et al.* 2005; Christopoulou *et al.* 2007; Doygun *et al.* 2008).

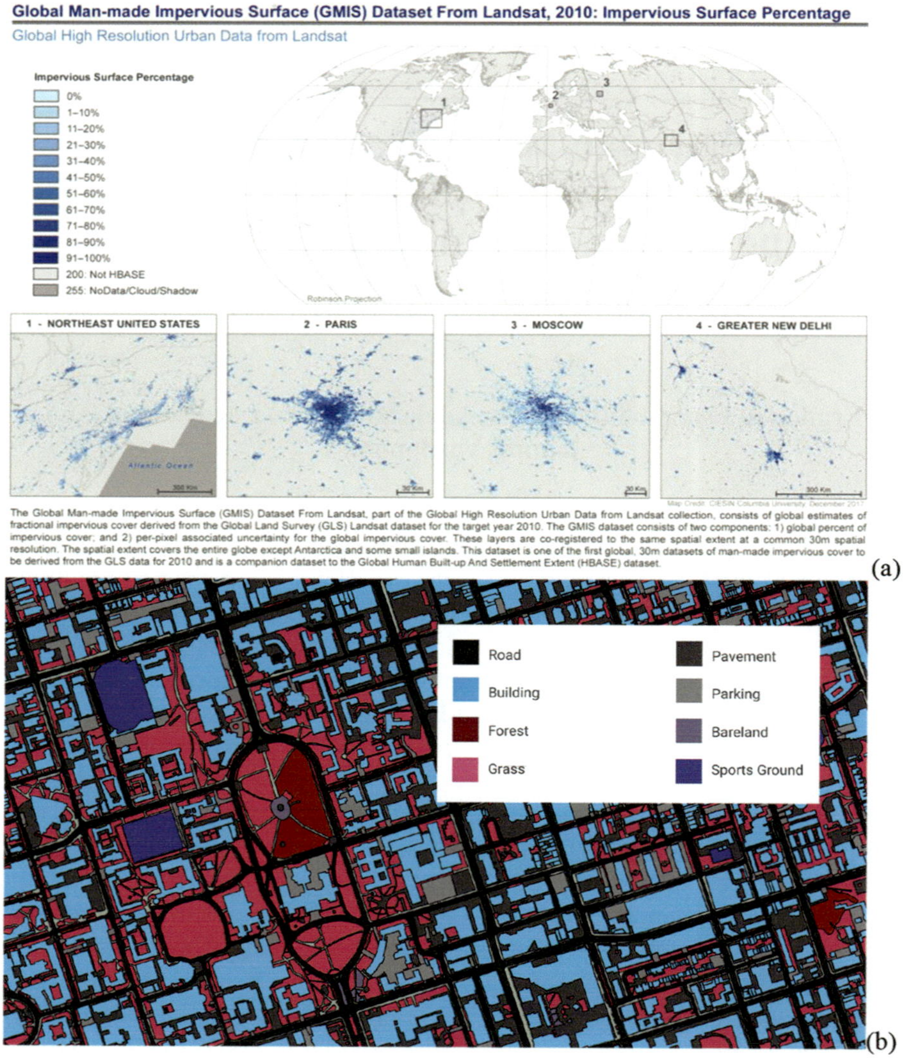

Figure 3.1 A global dataset providing detailed information about land cover, including impervious surfaces (a); a specific, local-scale map of soil sealing (b). (Attribution: EDACMaps, CC BY 2.0, via Wikimedia Commons).

This ongoing monitoring is instrumental in understanding the repercussions of escalating land imperviousness rates on landscape fragmentation, ecosystem health, and overall environmental quality (Figure 3.2). Such insights contribute to the sustainable planning of metropolitan regions (see Kempton *et al.*, 2022), aligning with the zero-net soil consumption target

Land take Compact city models Preferred land-use (on average): Pastures and fragmented agricultural areas around settlements, sometimes forests	Land take Dispersed city models Preferred land-use for urban conversion: Fragmented and unfragmented cropland (medium-high quality crop, wetlands)
Soil consumption Compact city models Preferred soil type (on average): Low-medium quality soils	Soil consumption Dispersed city models Preferred soil type (on average): Medium-high quality soils

Figure 3.2 Comparing different models of Mediterranean cities (left: compact settlements; right: dispersed settlements) as far as land take patterns and soil consumption trends are concerned. Source: Authors' own elaboration of literature data.

outlined in the Sustainable Development Goals of Agenda 2030 (Salvati and Carlucci, 2014).

Beneath the Surface: Exploring the Socio-Ecological Dynamics of Soil Sealing in Europe

To evaluate the effectiveness of land management strategies in soil protection, several indicators have been developed (Kilic *et al.* 2006; Catalàn *et al.* 2008; Schneider and Woodcock 2008; Salvati *et al.* 2012a). Unfortunately, computing official statistics, elementary variables, and topical indicators can be time-consuming. Moreover, the availability of data, particularly in emerging countries but sometimes also in advanced economies, may pose limitations (Table 3.1).

The 2001 National Land Cover Database of the United States, as detailed by Homer *et al.* (2004), incorporates an imperviousness layer alongside land cover and percent tree canopy layers. On the European front, the inaugural pan-European soil sealing database emerged during 2006–2008 as part of the Global Monitoring for Environment and Security (GMES) Fast Track Service on Land Monitoring. This database utilized multi-sensor and bi-temporal, ortho-rectified satellite imagery to generate a comprehensive map of land imperviousness coverage aligned with the continuous update of CORINE Land Cover maps (Figure 3.3). The European Environment Agency (EEA) has played a pivotal role in disseminating high-resolution maps of sealed soils, covering the entirety of Europe. These maps provide critical information for environmental monitoring at the regional level, with periodic updates in 2009, 2012, 2015, and 2018. Future updates are also scheduled in a relatively short time. Comparability across time and high spatial resolution

Table 3.1 The amount of per-capita built-up area (m^2) in Europe by country and year.

	Per-capita built-up area (m^2)				
Country	**2009**	**2012**	**2015**	**2018**	**Chg (2009–2018,%)**
Netherlands	431	457	472	457	0.7
Italy	440	459	472	484	1.1
United Kingdom	442	430	431	427	−0.4
Germany	527	553	565	587	1.3
Poland	532	594	624	634	2.1
Slovakia	538	515	536	632	1.9
Luxembourg	543	628	512	565	0.5
Spain	562	556	573	578	0.3
Greece	562	577	628	710	2.9
Belgium	573	538	582	584	0.2
Slovenia	579	571	609	625	0.9
Portugal	588	602	621	689	1.9
European Union (average)	*616*	*644*	*673*	*673*	*1.0*
Czechia	624	588	616	634	0.2
Austria	654	695	704	740	1.5
Hungary	703	681	704	812	1.7
France	834	841	835	845	0.1
Lithuania	899	804	1053	1091	2.4
Ireland	922	1016	961	973	0.6
Denmark	970	1021	1052	1054	1.0
Latvia	970	1127	1297	1276	3.5
Estonia	1164	1316	1541	1484	3.1
Sweden	1718	2084	2344	2223	3.3
Finland	2137	2338	2459	2448	1.6

Source: Authors' own elaboration and adaptation of European Environment Agency and Eurostat data.

are the major strengths of this key source for land imperviousness monitoring all over the old continent.

Building upon these foundations, the current study delves into the local-scale estimation of soil sealing rates, utilizing indicators derived from the previously mentioned maps. The objective is to offer a thorough evaluation encompassing various dimensions and implications of land imperviousness. This analysis takes into account habitat fragmentation, depletion of land quality, alterations in urban form, efficiency in urban land-uses, and the impact of exurban development – identified as potential consequences of a sudden surge in land imperviousness (see Table 3.2). The monitoring approach discussed in this study aims to be adaptable to diverse urban forms

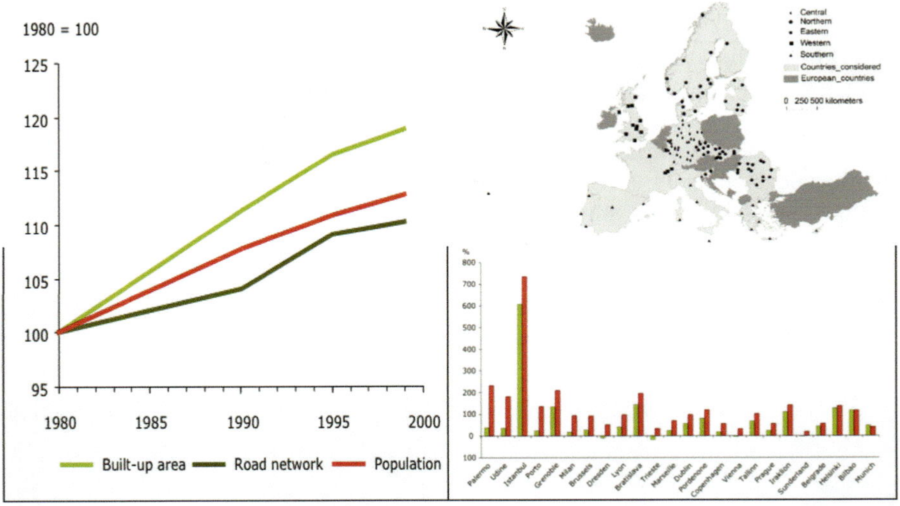

Figure 3.3 Stylized facts on the mismatch between population growth and urbanization in Europe (upper left: trends over time in the extent of built-up area, road network, and population in the old continent, by year; 1980 levels are illustrated as 100; upper right: the spatial distribution of surveyed cities divided by geographical region; lower right: annual rate of population growth (%) in a sample of cities along the last 10 years). Source: Authors' own elaboration and adaptation of Eurostat data and additional information from European Environment Agency.

and socioeconomic contexts. The insights gained from these approaches contribute to a broader discourse on potential strategies for mitigating soil sealing in suburban areas.

From Pixels to Patterns: Diving into Quantitative Measures of Land Imperviousness

A soil sealing map serves as a seamless raster layer, offering continuous percent values that represent the extent of land imperviousness (Luti *et al.*, 2020; Tombolini *et al.*, 2016). Impervious surfaces, including artificial structures like pavements (roads, sidewalks, driveways, and parking lots) covered with impermeable materials such as asphalt, concrete, brick, stone, and rooftops, are the primary components of this mapping (Figure 3.4). The degree of soil sealing, synonymous with the level of land imperviousness, is assessed based on pixel area (European Environment Agency, 2006).

In 2009, the EEA introduced a raster dataset illustrating built-up and non-built-up areas, presenting a continuous range of soil sealing rates from 0% to 100% (Munafò *et al.*, 2013). This dataset had an aggregated spatial

Table 3.2 Examples of operational dimensions and indicators of land imperviousness.

Operational dimension	Candidate indicator
Habitat fragmentation; impact on the hydrological cycle	Amount of pervious land
Efficiency in the use of land destined to urban development	Per-capita sealed land
Compact vs. dispersed urban form, land consumption	Intensity of soil sealing
Exurban development, soil quality, and land consumption	Diversification of the composition of sealed soils by degree of land imperviousness

Source: Authors' own elaboration on an extensive literature review.

Figure 3.4 A completely sealed parking land.

resolution of 100 × 100 m, derived from the spatial elaboration of an original layer product with a full spatial resolution of 20 × 20 m. This marked the commencement of the EEA's high-resolution land monitoring layer covering all of Europe. Subsequent updates to the imperviousness layers occurred at three-year intervals, allowing for an indirect quantification of human impact on agricultural and natural environments (Doukas *et al.*, 2023). The soil sealing data, encompassing 38 European countries, was derived from multi-sensor and bi-temporal, ortho-rectified satellite imagery (Salvati, 2014).

Validation of these maps involved the use of very high-resolution Google Earth imagery as an additional dataset. Reference sealing percentages were determined by employing a 10 × 10 m grid centered around sampling points. Classification accuracy assessment included estimating omission error, commission error, and overall accuracy. The classification accuracy for both built-up and non-built-up areas exceeded 85% per hectare (based on a 100 × 100 m grid), with both omission and commission errors below 15%. Based on the statistical information extracted from the map through descriptive analysis, approximately 6.5% of the European territory is covered by 1-hectare cells, exhibiting various degrees of sealing (ranging from 1% to 100%). The total sealed surface across the region amounts to 1.8%, and notably, a Mediterranean country like Greece ranks below the average with a sealing coverage of 1.3%.

Soil Sealing Dynamics in Mediterranean Europe – A Case Study

The enduring impact of diverse socioeconomic drivers, operating across elevation, coastal-inland, and metropolitan gradients, has intricately woven the tapestry of impervious land distribution in Southern Europe (Doukas *et al.*, 2022). Rooted in a millennial history of human settlement (Neuman, 2005), this phenomenon is particularly pronounced in coastal areas and flat districts, where recent years have witnessed a substantial surge in soil sealing rates. This surge is attributed to the expansive growth of large cities and the consolidation of medium-sized networks of rural settlements (Alphan 2003; Polyzos *et al.* 2008; Kucukmehmetoglu and Geymen 2009; Yilmaz 2010). This study delves into the consequential landscape transformations driven by urbanization, focusing on the spatial distribution of land imperviousness in metropolitan Athens, Greece, a mono-centric region nestled in Mediterranean Europe (D'Agata *et al.*, 2024).

Impervious land, spanning from 1% to 100%, constitutes 26% of the total investigated area, as illustrated in Figure 3.5. This concentration is particularly prominent in Athens' conurbation and the flat districts of Messoghia (east of Athens) and Thriasio (west of Athens). On a per-capita basis, impervious land averages to 200 m^2. The average land imperviousness, measured on a scale of soil sealing intensity from 0% to 100%, is 31%. The diversification of soil sealing intensity, assessed using the Pielou evenness index ranging from 0 (indicating the lowest diversification rate) to 1 (indicating the highest diversification rate), stands at 0.6. The maps and indicators collectively provide a comprehensive depiction of the level of land imperviousness in Attica. They illuminate fringe municipalities characterized by low land-use efficiency, marked by low-density dispersed settlements and high land

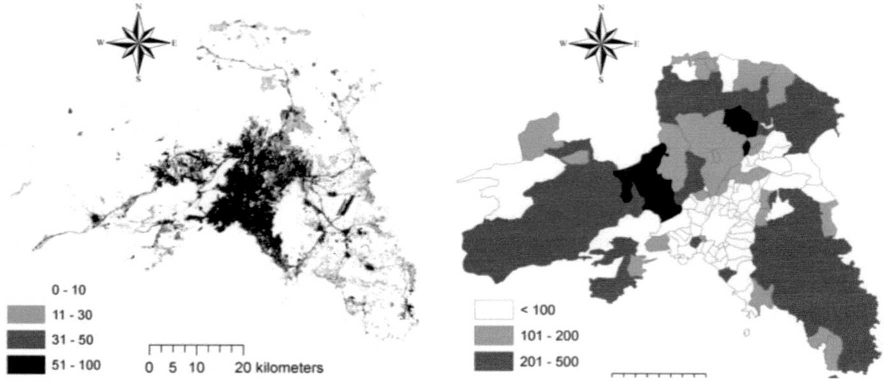

Figure 3.5 Map of metropolitan Athens illustrating the level of land imperviousness (left) and an elaboration integrating population census data to obtain a (small-scale) estimate of per-capita soil sealing rate (m^2) in the same area. Source: Authors own elaboration of Eurostat and ELSTAT data and additional information from European Environment Agency.

consumption. This stands in stark contrast to the more compact settlements in the downtown area and rural municipalities situated in peripheral locations (Vinci *et al.*, 2023; Lemonakis *et al.*, 2023).

The results unmistakably outline a spatial divide between urban municipalities, exhibiting a "sustainability footprint" characterized by dense settlements, high imperviousness degree, high sealing intensity, and low per-capita impervious land, and rural municipalities with a distinct footprint marked by low imperviousness degree, low sealing intensity, and high per capita impervious land. Fringe municipalities, demonstrating an intermediate sealing profile, vividly depict the process of urban spillover into rural land – a hallmark of Athens' development in recent decades (Couch *et al.*, 2007).

In regions experiencing deregulated urban expansion, the proliferation of low-density, dispersed settlements, especially evident in high-quality rural areas farther from the core city, contributes to a higher soil sealing intensity. This transformative process reflects the alteration of the landscape surrounding metropolitan regions into a rural-non-farm environment, with significant implications for soil quality and the potential exacerbation of land degradation (Allen, 2003; Alberti, 2005, 2010; Aguilar, 2008).

Balancing Act: Urbanization, Imperviousness, and Sustainable Planning

Empirical findings from the study highlight how models of urbanization and suburbanization exert distinct influences on land imperviousness. Specifically,

Figure 3.6 Partly sealed soils in close proximity to dispersed settlements in the outer fringe of Barcelona, Spain. Source: Authors' photographic archive.

exurban development induces a spatial reconfiguration of land-use along the urban–rural gradient, leading to higher rates of land consumption and lower per-capita soil occupation efficiency (Salvati and Vardopoulos, 2024). This transformation alters traditional landscape patterns and contributes to the fragmentation of high-quality plant cover (Alphan 2003; Paul and Tonts 2005; McGregor *et al.* 2006, Shahraki *et al.* 2011; Salvati *et al.* 2012b). The presence of second-home settlements intensifies land imperviousness, particularly along coastal and flat areas (Cuadrado-Ciuraneta *et al.*, 2016), where a pronounced surge in human pressure has been observed over the last three decades (Figure 3.6).

Despite soil sealing gaining recognition as a critical issue on the European policy agenda since the early 2000s (European Environment Agency, 2006), policies aimed at counteracting sprawl have proven only partially effective in Mediterranean Europe (Costa *et al.*, 1991; D'Agata *et al.*, 2023). A growing need exists for measures specifically tailored to address future settlement models, emphasizing the promotion of a "high-efficiency sealing profile" aligned with land-saving urban forms (Conway and Lathrop, 2005; Neuman, 2005; Torrens, 2006). Despite recent efforts, such as the master plan implemented in Athens (Nickayin *et al.*, 2020), which introduced measures to safeguard forests, green open lands, and agricultural areas surrounding the conurbation, their effectiveness in containing sprawl remains limited (Chorianopoulos *et al.*, 2010).

Furthermore, the rapid development of suburbs has the potential to reshape residents' perceptions of environmental vulnerability and soil resource depletion (Vinci *et al.*, 2021). Simultaneously, public officials and local stakeholders may persist in viewing landscape conservation and environmental degradation as exclusively agricultural- or forest-related issues (Reckien *et al.*, 2011). This dynamic is especially pertinent in regions where urban–rural divides are starkly apparent. Sustainable planning strategies should play a pivotal role in prompting a reconsideration of prevailing urban forms, steering them toward greater sustainability (Vardopoulos *et al.*, 2023). Land-use maps may represent the necessary information base to this pivotal policy implementation (Figure 3.7).

To conclude, this study illustrates how simplified, small-scale indicators derived from high-resolution imperviousness layers can offer valuable insights into the analysis of urbanization-driven soil sealing, carrying implications for urban containment policies. Through a quantitative analysis of the distribution of land imperviousness classes, these indicators unveil a "soil sealing footprint" for each municipality within a given metropolitan region. This footprint is correlated with factors such as the socioeconomic profile, territorial and planning constraints, as well as the environmental and ecological background. Distinct municipal types, such as strictly urban, intermediate, and strictly rural, can be identified based on their unique land imperviousness and socioeconomic profiles. Strictly rural municipalities exhibit a relatively low soil sealing intensity and a medium–low diversity of land imperviousness classes. Interestingly, there is a moderately positive correlation between soil sealing intensity and the diversity of land imperviousness classes in these areas.

Conversely, strictly urban municipalities exhibit a negative correlation between soil sealing intensity and the diversification of land imperviousness classes. Proximity to rural areas does not preclude suburban municipalities from undergoing rapid territorial transformations, manifesting in a distinctive soil sealing profile. Intermediate municipalities, encompassing recently urbanized areas characterized by low-density, dispersed settlements, represent regions undergoing recent suburbanization. These areas exhibit the highest sealing intensity, the lowest sealing efficiency, and the highest diversification in sealing profiles. These intermediate areas emerge as "land imperviousness" hotspots, suggesting the need for specific measures

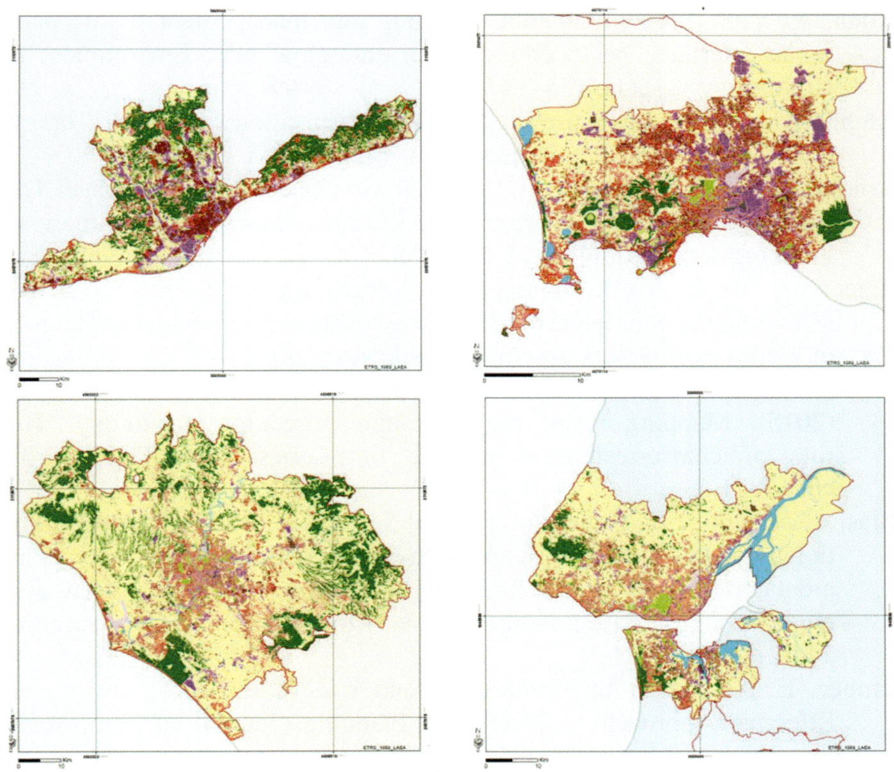

Figure 3.7 Envisaging present and future land-use of the Mediterranean cities: the basic contribution of Urban Atlas (upper left: Barcelona; upper right: Naples; lower left: Rome; lower right: Lisbon). Source: Authors' own adaptation of European Environment Agency data.

aimed at containing sprawl. This aligns with the commitment of the Agenda 2030 Sustainable Development Goals concerning sustainable cities and regions.

References

Aguilar, A.G., (2008). Peri-urbanization, illegal settlements and environmental impact in Mexico City. Cities, 25, 133–145.

Alberti, M., (2005). The Effects of Urban Patterns on Ecosystem Function. International Regional Science Review, 28(2), 168–192.

Alberti, M., (2010). Maintaining ecological integrity and sustaining ecosystem function in urban areas. Current Opinion in Environmental Sustainability, 2(3), 178–184.

Allen, A., (2003). Environmental planning and management of the peri-urban interface: perspectives on an emerging field. Environment & Urbanization, 15(1), 135–147.

Alphan, H. (2003). Land use change and urbanisation of Adana, Turkey. Land Degradation and Development, 14, 575–586.

Arnold, C. L., and Gibbons, C. J. (1996). Impervious Surface Coverage: The Emergence of a Key Environmental Indicator. Journal of the American Planning Association, 62(2), 243–258.

Bajocco, S., Ceccarelli, T., Smiraglia, D., Salvati, L., and Ricotta, C. (2016). Modeling the ecological niche of long-term land use changes: The role of biophysical factors. Ecological Indicators, 60, 231–236.

Bajocco, S., Dragoz, E., Gitas, I., Smiraglia, D., Salvati, L., and Ricotta, C. (2015). Mapping forest fuels through vegetation phenology: The role of coarse-resolution satellite time-series. PloS One, 10(3), e0119811.

Biasi, R., Brunori, E., Smiraglia, D., and Salvati, L. (2015). Linking traditional tree-crop landscapes and agro-biodiversity in Central Italy using a database of typical and traditional products: A multiple risk assessment through a data mining analysis. Biodiversity and Conservation, 24(12), 3009–3031.

Brabec, E. A. (2009). Imperviousness and Land-Use Policy: Toward an Effective Approach to Watershed Planning. Journal of Hydrologic Engineering, 14(4), 425–433.

Byrne, L. B., (2007). Habitat structure: a fundamental concept and framework for urban soil ecology. Urban Ecosystems, 10, 255–274.

Carlucci, M., Chelli, F.M., and Salvati, L. (2018). Toward a new cycle: Short-term population dynamics, gentrification, and re-urbanization of Milan (Italy). Sustainability, 10(9), 3014.

Catalàn, B., Sauri, D. and Serra, P., (2008). Urban sprawl in the Mediterranean? Patterns of growth and change in the Barcelona Metropolitan Region 1993–2000. Landscape and Urban Planning, 85(3–4), 174–184.

Cecchini, M., Zambon, I., Pontrandolfi, A., Turco, R., Colantoni, A., Mavrakis, A., and Salvati, L. (2019). Urban sprawl and the ‘olive’ landscape: Sustainable land management for ‘crisis’ cities. GeoJournal, 84(1), 237–255.

Cecchini, M., Zambon, I., Pontrandolfi, A., Turco, R., Colantoni, A., Mavrakis, A., and Salvati, L. (2019). Urban sprawl and the ‘olive’ landscape: Sustainable land management for ‘crisis’ cities. GeoJournal, 84(1), 237–255.

Chelleri, L., Schuetze, T., and Salvati, L. (2015). Integrating resilience with urban sustainability in neglected neighborhoods: Challenges and opportunities of transitioning to decentralized water management in Mexico City. Habitat International, 48, 122–130.

Chianucci, F., Puletti, N., Grotti, M., Bisaglia, C., Giannetti, F., Romano, E., Brambilla, M., Mattioli, W., Cabassi, G., Bajocco, S., Li, L., Chirici, G., Corona, P., and Tattoni C. (2021). Influence of image pixel resolution on canopy cover estimation in poplar plantations from field, aerial and satellite optical imagery. Annals of Silvicultural Research, 46(1), 8–13.

Chirici, G., Giannetti, F., McRoberts, R., Travaglini, D., Pecchi, M., Maselli, F., Chiesi, M., and Corona, P. (2020). Wall-to-wall spatial prediction of growing stock volume based on Italian National Forest Inventory plots and remotely sensed data. International Journal of Applied Earth Observation and Geoinformation, 84, 101959.

Chorianopoulos, I., Pagonis, T., Koukoulas, S. and Drymoniti, S. (2010). Planning, competitiveness and sprawl in the Mediterranean city: The case of Athens. Cities, 27, 249–259.

Christopoulou, O., Polyzos, S. and Minetos, D., (2007). Peri-urban and urban forests in Greece: obstacle or advantage to urban development? Journal of Environmental Management, 18, 382–395.

Ciommi, M., Chelli, F. M., Carlucci, M., and Salvati, L. (2018). Urban growth and demographic dynamics in southern Europe: Toward a new statistical approach to regional science. Sustainability, 10(8), 2765.

Ciommi, M., Chelli, F.M., and Salvati, L. (2019). Integrating parametric and non-parametric multivariate analysis of urban growth and commuting patterns in a European metropolitan area. Quality & Quantity, 53(2), 957–979.

Conway, T. M. and Lathrop, R. G., (2005). Alternative land-use regulations and environmental impacts: assessing future land-use in an urbanizing watershed. Landscape and Urban Planning, 71(1), 1–15.

Corona, P. (2018). Communicating facts, findings and thinking to support evidence-based strategies and decisions. Annals of Silvicultural Research, 42, 1–2.

Corona, P. (2019). Global change and silvicultural research. Annals of Silvicultural Research, 43(1), 1–3.

Corona, P., Cutini, A., Chiavetta, U., and Paoletti, E. (2016). Forest-food nexus: a topical opportunity for human well-being and silviculture. Annals of Silvicultural Research, 40(1), 1–10.

Costa, F. J., Noble, A. G. and Pendeleton, G., (1991). Evolving planning systems in Madrid, Rome, and Athens. Geojournal, 24(3), 293–303.

Couch, C., Petschel-held, G. and Leontidou, L. (2007). Urban Sprawl In Europe: Landscapes, Land-use Change and Policy. London: Blackwell.

Cuadrado-Ciuraneta, S., Durà-Guimerà, A., and Salvati, L. (2017). Not only tourism: unravelling suburbanization, second-home expansion and "rural" sprawl in Catalonia, Spain. Urban Geography, 38(1), 66–89.

D'Agata, A., Nosova, B., Vardopoulos, I., Rontos, K., Clemente, M., Colombo, C., Sateriano, A., and Salvati, L. (2024). Urban decline, Economic crisis and fringe landscapes: The Mediterranean experience. In A. Sateriano (Ed.), Urban Crisis: Social and Economic Implications for Southern Europe. Nova Science: Hauppauge, NY, USA. ISBN: 979-8-89113-242-9.

D'Agata, A., Ponza, D., Stroiu, F. A., Vardopoulos, I., Rontos, K., Escrivà, F., Chelli, F., Alaimo, L. S., Salvati, L., and Nickyain, S. S. (2023). Toward sustainable development trajectories? Estimating urban footprints from high-resolution copernicus layers in Athens, Greece. Land, 12(8), 1490.

De Marco, A., Proietti, C., Anav, A., Ciancarella, L., D'Elia, I., Fares, S., Fornasier, M.F., Fusaro, L., Gualtieri, M., Manes, F., Marchetto, A., Mircea, M., Paoletti, E., Piersanti, A., Rogora, M., Salvati, L., Salvatori, E., Screpanti, A., Vialetto, G., Vitale, M., and Leonardi, C. (2019). Impacts of air pollution on human and ecosystem health, and implications for the National Emission Ceilings Directive: Insights from Italy. Environment International, 125, 320–333.

Delfanti, L., Colantoni, A., Recanatesi, F., Bencardino, M., Sateriano, A., Zambon, I., and Salvati, L. (2016). Solar plants, environmental degradation and local socioeconomic contexts: A case study in a Mediterranean country. Environmental Impact Assessment Review, 61, 88–93.

Di Feliciantonio, C., Salvati, L., Sarantakou, E., and Rontos, K. (2018). Class diversification, economic growth and urban sprawl: Evidences from a pre-crisis European city. Quality & Quantity, 52(4), 1501–1522.

Doukas, Y. E., Maravegias, N., and Andreou, G. (Eds.). (2022). Η χωρική διάσταση της ευρωπαϊκής ολοκλήρωσης: σύγκλιση ή απόκλιση; Dionicos: Athens, Greece. ISBN: 978-6185-6650-3-6.

Doukas, Y. E., Salvati, L., and Vardopoulos, I. (2023). Unraveling the European Agricultural Policy Sustainable Development Trajectory. Land, 12(9), 1749.

Doygun, H., Alphan, H. and Gurun, D. K. (2008). Analysing urban expansion and land use suitability for the city of Kahramanmaras, Turkey, and its surrounding region. Environmental Monitoring and Assessment, 145, 387–395.

Duvernoy, I., Zambon, I., Sateriano, A., and Salvati, L. (2018). Pictures from the other side of the fringe: Urban growth and peri-urban agriculture in a post-industrial city (Toulouse, France). Journal of Rural Studies, 57, 25–35.

Economidou, E., (1993). The Attic landscape throughout the centuries and its human degradation. Landscape and Urban Planning, 24, 33–37.

European Environment Agency, (2010). Mapping guide for a European urban atlas. Version 1.1. Copenhagen: EEA.

European Environmental Agency, (2006). Urban sprawl in Europe – The ignored challenge. Copenhagen: EEA Report no. 10.

Fares, S., Bajocco, S., Salvati, L., Camarretta, N., Dupuis, J. L., Xanthopoulos, G., Guijarro, M., Madrigal, J., Hernando, C., and Corona P. (2017). Characterizing potential wildland fire fuel in live vegetation in the Mediterranean region. Annals of Forest Science, 74, 1–12.

Garcia, D. and Riera, P., (2003). Expansion versus density in Barcelona: a valuation exercise. Urban Studies, 40(10), 1925–1936.

Gavalas, V.S., Rontos, K., and Salvati, L. (2014). Who becomes an unwed mother in Greece? Sociodemographic and geographical aspects of an emerging phenomenon. Population, Space and Place, 20(3), 250–263.

Giannakourou, G., (2005). Transforming spatial planning policy in Mediterranean countries: Europeanization and domestic change. European Planning Studies, 13, 319–331.

Homer, C., Huang, C., Yang, L., Wylie, B. and Coan, M., (2004). Development of a 2001 National Land-Cover Database for the United States. Photogrammetric Engineering and Remote Sensing, 70(7), 829–840.

Inglezakis, V., and Zorpas, A. A. (2014). Environmental indicators. In A. A. Zorpas (Ed.), Sustainability behind Sustainability, (pp. 17–33). Hauppauge, New York, USA. Nova Science Publishers.

Johnson, M. P., (2001). Environmental impacts of urban sprawl: a survey of the literature and proposed research agenda. Environment and Planning A, 33(4), 717–735.

Kempton, Y., Salvati, L., and Vardopoulos, I. (2022). Long-term planning and development for urban and regional inclusion, safety, resilience, and sustainability. Insights from Singapore. Region & Periphery, 14(10), 58–78.

Kilic, S., Evrendilek, F., Berberoglu, S. and Demirkesen, A. C., (2006). Environmental monitoring of land-use and land-cover changes in a Mediterranean region of Turkey. Environmental Monitoring and Assessment, 114, 157–168.

Kosmas, C., Karamesouti, M., Kounalaki, K., Detsis, V., Vassiliou, P., and Salvati, L. (2016). Land degradation and long-term changes in agro-pastoral systems: An empirical analysis of ecological resilience in Asteroussia-Crete (Greece). Catena, 147, 196–204.

Kucukmehmetoglu, M. and Geymen, A. (2009). Urban sprawl factors in the surface water resource basins of Istanbul. Land Use Policy, 26, 569–579.

Lamonica, G.R., Recchioni, M.C., Chelli, F.M., and Salvati, L. (2020). The efficiency of the cross-entropy method when estimating the technical coefficients of input–output tables. Spatial Economic Analysis, 15(1), 62–91.

Lee, J. G., and Heaney, J. P. (2003). Estimation of Urban Imperviousness and its Impacts on Storm Water Systems. Journal of Water Resources Planning and Management, 129(5), 419–426.

Lemonakis, C., Alexopoulos, G., Garefalakis, A., and Garefalakis, S. (2024). Trends and new elements in urban hierarchy research: the Greek paradigm. The Annals of Regional Science, 72, 335–354.

Luti, T., Segoni, S., Catani, F., Munafò, M., and Casagli, N. (2020). Integration of Remotely Sensed Soil Sealing Data in Landslide Susceptibility Mapping. Remote Sensing, 12(9), 1486.

McGregor, D., Simon, D. and Thompson, D. (2006). The peri-urban interface: approaches to sustainable natural and human resource use. London: Earthscan.

Miller, J. D., Kim, H., Kjeldsen, T. R., Packman, J., Grebby, S., and Dearden, R. (2014). Assessing the impact of urbanization on storm runoff in a peri-urban catchment using historical change in impervious cover. Journal of Hydrology, 515, 59–70.

Munafò, M., Norero, C., Sabbi, A. and Salvati, L. (2010). Urban soil consumption in the growing city: a survey in Rome. Scottish Geographical Journal, 126(3), 153–161.

Munafò, M., Salvati, L., and Zitti, M. (2013). Estimating soil sealing rate at national level—Italy as a case study. Ecological Indicators, 26, 137–140.

Neuman, M., (2005). The compact city fallacy. Journal of Planning and Education Research, 25(1), 11–26.

Nickayin, S. S., Tomao, A., Quaranta, G., Salvati, L., and Gimenez Morera, A. (2020). Going toward Resilience? Town Planning, Peri-Urban Landscapes, and the Expansion of Athens, Greece. Sustainability, 12(24), 10471.

Nocentini S., Buttoud G., Ciancio O., and Corona P. (2017). Managing forests in a changing world: the need for a systemic approach. A review. Forest Systems, 26(1), eR01.

Paul, V. and Tonts, M. (2005). Containing urban sprawl: trends in land-use and spatial planning in the Metropolitan Region of Barcelona. Journal of Environmental Planning and Management, 48(1), 7–35.

Perrin, C., Nougarèdes, B., Sini, L., Branduini, P., and Salvati, L. (2018). Governance changes in peri-urban farmland protection following decentralisation: A comparison between Montpellier (France) and Rome (Italy). Land Use Policy, 70, 535–546.

Poelmans, L., Van Rompaey, A. and Batelaan, O. (2010). Coupling urban expansion models and hydrological models: how important are spatial patterns? Land Use Policy, 27, 965–975.

Polyzos, S., Christopoulou, O., Minetos, D., and Leal Filho, W. (2008). An overview of urban-rural land use interactions in Greece. International Journal of Agricultural Resources, Governance and Ecology, 7, 276–296.

Recanatesi, F., Clemente, M., Grigoriadis, E., Ranalli, F., Zitti, M., and Salvati, L. (2016). A fifty-year sustainability assessment of Italian agro-forest districts. Sustainability, 8(1), 32.

Reckien, D., Eisenack, K. and Ludeke, K. B. (2011). Land consumption by urban sprawl - a new approach to deduce urban development scenarios from actors' preferences. Environmental Modeling and Assessment, 16, 465–477.

Rondeux, J., Bertini, R., Bastrup-Birk, A., Corona, P., Latte, N., McRoberts, R.E., Ståhl, G., Winter, S., and Chirici G. (2012). Assessing deadwood using harmonized national forest inventory data. Forest Science, 58, 269–283.

Salvati, L. (2014). The spatial pattern of soil sealing along the urban-rural gradient in a Mediterranean region. Journal of Environmental Planning and Management, 57(6), 848–861.

Salvati, L. (2014). Towards a Polycentric Region? The Socio-economic Trajectory of Rome, an 'Eternally Mediterranean' City. Tijdschrift voor Economische en Sociale Geografie, 105(3), 268–284.

Salvati, L. and Zitti, M. (2011). Economic growth vs land quality: a multi-dimensional approach in Italy. Journal of Environmental Planning and Management, 54(6), 733–748.

Salvati, L., and Carlucci, M. (2014). Zero Net Land Degradation in Italy: The role of socioeconomic and agro-forest factors. Journal of Environmental Management, 145, 299–306.

Salvati, L., and Carlucci, M. (2016). Patterns of Sprawl: The Socioeconomic and Territorial Profile of Dispersed Urban Areas in Italy. Regional Studies, 50(8), 1346–1359.

Salvati, L., and Ricciardo Lamonica, G. (2020). Containing urban expansion: Densification vs greenfield development, socio-demographic transformations and the economic crisis in a Southern European City, 2006–2015. Ecological Indicators, 110, 105923.

Salvati, L., and Zitti, M. (2007). Territorial disparities, natural resource distribution, and land degradation: a case study in southern Europe. Geojournal, 70(2), 185–194.

Salvati, L., and Zitti, M. (2009). Substitutability and weighting of ecological and economic indicators: Exploring the importance of various components of a synthetic index. Ecological Economics, 68(4), 1093–1099.

Salvati, L., and Vardopoulos, I. (2024). Intricacies of Mediterranean urban and regional dynamics. Euro-Mediterranean Journal for Environmental Integration, in press.

Salvati, L., Ciommi, M. T., Serra, P., and Chelli, F. M. (2019). Exploring the spatial structure of housing prices under economic expansion and stagnation: The role of socio-demographic factors in metropolitan Rome, Italy. Land Use Policy, 81, 143–152.

Salvati, L., Ferrara, A., and Chelli, F. (2018). Long-term growth and metropolitan spatial structures: An analysis of factors influencing urban patch size under different economic cycles. Geografisk Tidsskrift - Danish Journal of Geography, 118(1), 56–71.

Salvati, L., Gemmiti, R., and Perini, L. (2012). Land degradation in Mediterranean urban areas: an unexplored link with planning? Area, 44(3), 317–325.

Salvati, L., Petitta, M., Ceccarelli, T., Perini, L., Di Battista, F., and Scarascia, M.E.V. (2008). Italy's renewable water resources as estimated on the basis of the monthly water balance. Irrigation and Drainage: The journal of the International Commission on Irrigation and Drainage, 57(5), 507–515.

Salvati, L., Zitti, M., and Sateriano, A. (2013). Changes in city vertical profile as an indicator of sprawl: Evidence from a Mediterranean urban region. Habitat International, 38, 119–125.

Scalenghe, R., and Marsan, F. A. (2009). The anthropogenic sealing of soils in urban areas. Landscape and Urban Planning, 90(1–2), 1–10.

Schneider, A. and Woodcock, C. E. (2008). Compact, dispersed, fragmented, extensive? A comparison of urban growth in twenty-five global cities using remotely sensed data, pattern metrics and census information. Urban Studies, 45(3), 659–692.

Shahraki, S. Z., Sauri, D., Serra, P., Modugno, S., Seifolddini, F. and Pourahmad, A. (2011). Urban sprawl pattern and land-use change detection in Yazd, Iran. Habitat International, 35, 521–528.

Smiraglia, D., Ceccarelli, T., Bajocco, S., Perini, L., and Salvati, L. (2015). Unraveling Landscape Complexity: Land Use/Land Cover Changes and Landscape Pattern Dynamics (1954–2008) in Contrasting Peri-Urban and Agro-Forest Regions of Northern Italy. Environmental Management, 56(4), 916–932.

Tombolini, I., Munafò, M., and Salvati, L. (2016). Soil sealing footprint as an indicator of dispersed urban growth: a multivariate statistics approach. Urban Research & Practice, 9(1), 1–15.

Torrens, P. M. (2006). Simulating sprawl. Annals of the Association of American Geographers, 96(2), 248–275.

Tsai, Y. (2005). Quantifying urban form: compactness versus sprawl. Urban Studies, 42(1), 141–161.

Vardopoulos, I., and Karytsas, S. (2019). An exploratory path analysis of climate change effects on tourism. Sustainable Development, Culture, Traditions Journal, Special Volume in Honor of Professor George I. Theodoropoulos, 132–152.

Vardopoulos, I., Ioannides, S., Georgiou, M., Voukkali, I., Salvati, L., and Doukas, Y. E. (2023). Shaping sustainable cities: A long-rerm GIS-emanated spatial analysis of settlement growth and planning in a coastal Mediterranean European city. Sustainability, 15(14), 11202

Vinci, S., Egidi, G., Salvia, R., Gimenez Morera, A., and Salvati, L. (2022). Natural population growth and urban management in metropolitan regions: Insights from pre-crisis and post-crisis Athens, Greece. Urban Studies, 59(12), 2527–2544.

Vinci, S., Vardopoulos, I., and Salvati, L. (2023). A tale of a shrinking City? Exploring the complex interplay of socio-demographic dynamics in the recent development of Attica, Greece. Cities, 132, 104089.

Weber, C., Petropoulou, C. and Hirsch, J. (2005). Urban development in the Athens metropolitan area using remote sensing data with supervised analysis and GIS. International Journal of Remote Sensing, 26(4), 785–796.

Wessolek, G. (2008). Sealing of Soils. In Urban Ecology (pp. 161–179). Springer US.

Yilmaz, R. (2010). Monitoring land use/land cover changes using CORINE land cover data: a case study of Silivri coastal zone in metropolitan Istanbul. Environmental Monitoring and Assessment, 165, 603–615.

Zambon, I., Benedetti, A., Ferrara, C., and Salvati, L. (2018). Soil matters? A multivariate analysis of socioeconomic constraints to urban expansion in Mediterranean Europe. Ecological Economics, 146, 173–183.

Zambon, I., Colantoni, A., Carlucci, M., Morrow, N., Sateriano, A., and Salvati, L. (2017). Land quality, sustainable development and environmental degradation in agricultural districts: A computational approach based on entropy indexes. Environmental Impact Assessment Review, 64, 37–46.

4

Deciphering Metropolitan Expansion: Settlement Patterns and Socio-Environmental Dynamics

Ioannis Vardopoulos, Francisco Escrivà Saneugenio, Adele Sateriano, and Luca Salvati

Metropolitan expansion has significantly influenced the spatial dynamics between urban and non-urban land-use, giving rise to heterogeneous fringes that blend compact and dispersed settlements (Vardopoulos *et al.*, 2023). This has resulted in a spatially discontinuous form of urbanization, carrying negative socioeconomic and environmental consequences (Heim, 2001; Hasse and Lathrop, 2003; Hewitt and Escobar, 2011). The transformation of fringes has contributed to the fragmentation of relict landscapes, impacting agricultural and forested areas, which are progressively losing their ability to act as buffers against unregulated urban expansion (Salvati *et al.*, 2014; Maravegias and Doukas, 2012).

This, in turn, poses challenges in preserving fertile soils from real estate speculation (Allen, 2003; Aguilar, 2008; Baing, 2010). As these processes drive spatially imbalanced development (Colantoni *et al.*, 2015; Doukas *et al.*, 2022), there is a growing need for regional planning to redirect current forms of metropolitan expansion toward urban containment and settlement compaction (Thinh *et al.*, 2002; Turok and Mykhnenko, 2007; Cuadrado-Ciuraneta *et al.*, 2017).

Cities in advanced economies have undergone expansion in diverse economic conditions and settlement contexts, resulting in multifaceted development paths (Forster, 2006; Gennaio *et al.*, 2009; Halleux *et al.*, 2012). Despite marked spatial heterogeneity, two dominant models have emerged: (i) radio-centric growth (Mitoula and Papavasileiou, 2023; D'Agata *et al.*, 2024), fostering urban compactness (Vardopoulos *et al.*, 2023), and (ii) a progressive shift toward urban dispersion (D'Agata *et al.*, 2023), leading to spatially discontinuous settlement expansion (Couch *et al.*, 2005; D'Agata *et al.*, 2023).

Demographic growth has been a driving force behind radio-centric urban expansion (Cheshire and Magrini, 2009; Vinci *et al.*, 2023). In contrast, globalized economic development, decentralization processes, land speculation, and laissez-faire planning regulations have fueled a more dispersed pattern of growth in affluent countries (Oueslati *et al.*, 2015; Weilenmann *et al.*, 2017; Zambon *et al.*, 2017). Within the current metropolitan context, there is a call for mixed (qualitative–quantitative) approaches that can identify and respond to new forms of urbanization (Wissen Hayek *et al.*, 2011). This is crucial, as traditional research perspectives deeply ingrained in planning systems are considered "inadequate for dealing with processes of environmental and developmental change in the peri-urban context" (Allen, 2003; Lemonakis *et al.*, 2023).

By delineating the "distinctive peri-urban challenges of appropriate and flexible planning and development" (Simon, 2008), a nuanced analysis of the intricate structure of urban landscapes should concentrate on settlement compactness and dispersion processes (D'Agata *et al.*, 2023; Vardopoulos *et al.*, 2023). This involves proposing indicators that contribute significantly to both positive advancements and normative improvements (Frenkel, 2004; Hongling and Teng, 2013; Ceccarelli *et al.*, 2014).

Utilizing simplified indicators, a diachronic (micro-scale) investigation of the neighboring configuration of buildings (Figure 4.1) can offer informed insights into long-term and short-term trends in urban compactness and dispersion (Kazemzadeh-Zow *et al.*, 2017). With this perspective, building censuses provide fully comparable, freely available, spatially accurate, and temporally reliable indicators (Corona, 2018, 2019), considered suitable for a broad range of applications and empirical exercises that inform urban science and regional planning (Salvati, 2016).

Empirical analyses introduce simplified indicator of settlement compactness based on the evolution over time of the number of detached buildings in the total stock at a sufficiently detailed geographical scale (Martinuzzi *et al.*, 2007). Shifting away from traditional perspectives grounded in the analysis of land-use toward a more refined approach that focuses on settlement structure and building neighboring regimes may reconnect morphological analyses of urban fabric with a functional characterization of metropolitan regions (Salvati *et al.*, 2016; Pili *et al.*, 2017; Duvernoy *et al.*, 2018).

In the present contribution, the modalities of settlement expansion are posited as strictly dependent on the interplay among local economic functions, social aspects, territorial constraints, and planning regulations (Couch

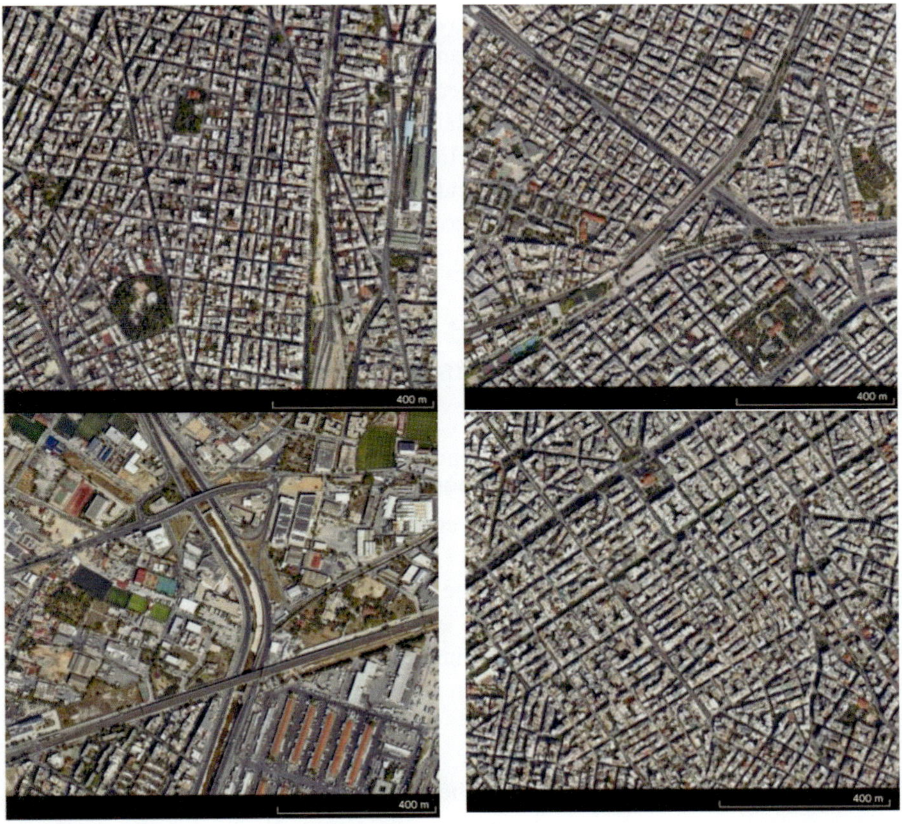

Figure 4.1 The compact urban footprint in the Greater Athens' area: upper left: mixed residential–industrial settlements in Kolonos–Sepolia, upper right: mixed residential–commercial settlements in Tavros–Kallithea, lower left: purely service settlements in Agios Ioannis Renti, and lower right: purely residential settlements in Pangrati. Source: Authors' own elaboration on Google Earth imagery.

et al., 2007; D'Agata *et al.*, 2024b). In this context, a more comprehensive characterization of the socioeconomic mechanisms underlying compact versus dispersed urban expansion contributes to a "holistic" understanding of contemporary urbanization processes, connecting urban form with metropolitan functions on a broader scale (European Environment Agency, 2006).

More specifically, discerning the spatial dynamics of compact/dispersed urban expansion and understanding the underlying contextual background informs effective strategies for the sustainable management of fringe land (Jabareen, 2006; Jaeger *et al.*, 2010; Lauf *et al.*, 2016; D' Agata *et al.*, 2024). These strategies should increasingly align with a place-specific "urban containment" philosophy (Hoymann, 2011). By hypothesizing that the effectiveness of urban containment strategies depends on the intrinsic characteristics of local contexts (Gil *et al.*, 2020; Ragazou *et al.*, 2022), the current study evaluates the spatial relationship between compactness trends and socioeconomic impulses (Di Feliciantonio and Salvati, 2015), taking into account the intrinsic role of local contexts and estimating the impact of (municipal) town planning in the context of deregulated urban expansion (Giannakourou, 2005).

In-between Compactness and Dispersion: Socioeconomic Factors, Territorial Constraints, and Planning Regulations Shaping Settlements

Southern Europe stands out as a paradigmatic area where dispersed urban expansion has solidified since the 1990s, driven by spatial decentralization policies and shifts in lifestyles that encourage short-haul mobility toward suburban regions (Carlucci *et al.*, 2017). With unregulated land development driving settlement expansion until the 1980s, exurban development in the Mediterranean has undergone rapid changes toward spatially discontinuous growth (Figure 4.2), resulting in land consumption and various negative environmental implications (Orenstein and Hamburg, 2010; Ceccarelli *et al.*, 2014; Colantoni *et al.*, 2016).

Building upon these premises, the Mediterranean region provides a promising context for evaluating the primary drivers of settlement compactness or dispersion and the underlying determinants at both the local and regional scales (Salvati and Serra, 2016). From this perspective, local administrative units, specifically municipalities, are considered appropriate spatial domains for analysis (Salvati *et al.*, 2017). Municipalities are empowered to prepare, approve, and enforce town master plans, make decisions on land-use, and assess alternative developmental opportunities (Zambon *et al.*, 2018).

While the role of boundaries in characterizing metropolitan forms and functions is still not fully understood, it is recognized as decisive (Paul and Tonts, 2005; Ningal *et al.*, 2008; Kim *et al.*, 2015). The international community has taken note of this issue, especially in the context of the recent debate on more sustainable urban forms for metropolitan regions (Cheshire and Magrini, 2009; Paulsen, 2013; Oueslati *et al.*, 2015). Despite these considerations, spatially explicit land-use approaches that involve a quantitative analysis of the micro-scale evolution of settlement structures (*e.g.*, evaluating building borders and contact elements) are relatively uncommon in planning science (*e.g.*, Rahimi, 2016; Vardopoulos, 2023). Recent studies, however,

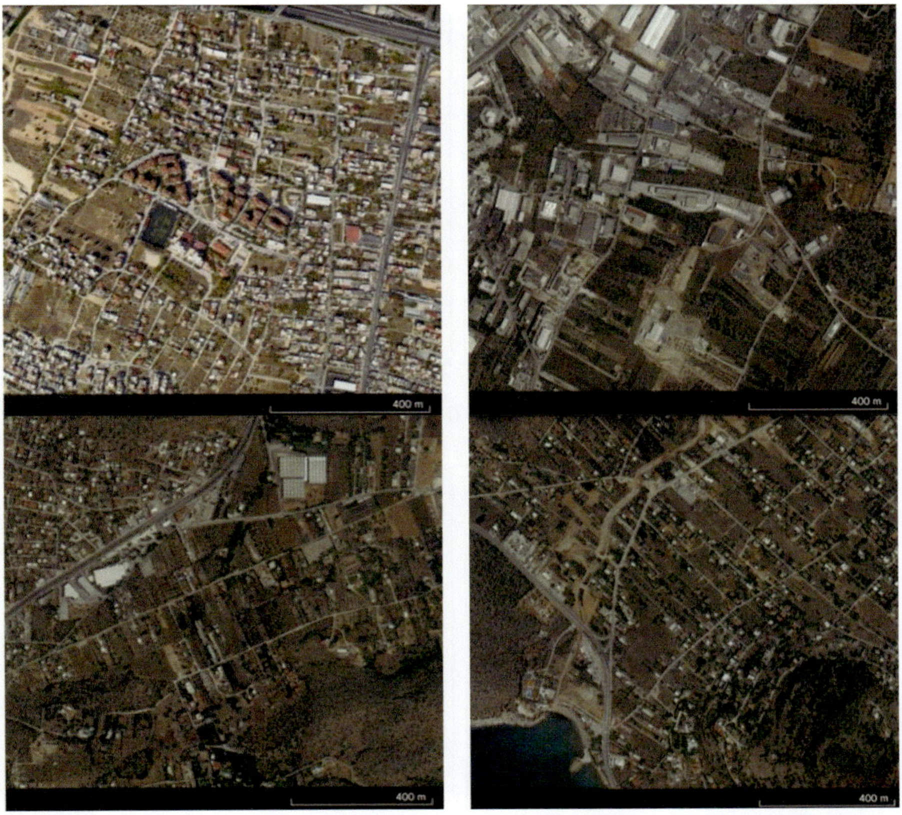

Figure 4.2 The dispersed urban footprint in metropolitan Athens: upper left: mixed residential-service settlements in Kato Acharnes-Zefiri, upper right: industrial–commercial settlements in Koropi; lower left: mixed industrial–residential settlements in Vari, and lower right: second-home settlements in Lagonisi. Source: Authors' own elaboration on Google Earth imagery.

have started to conceptualize the "boundary" notion in spatial governance by designating clear limits for homogeneous districts and land-use classes (Zhang, 2001; Salvati *et al.*, 2018).

Undertaking a comprehensive review and analysis of existing empirical studies for the Athens' metropolitan region – a representative case for Mediterranean Europe (Vardopoulos and Theodoropoulou, 2019) – this study has benefited from various integrated analyses grounded in multivariate statistics and spatially explicit regression techniques (*e.g.*, Grekousis *et al.*, 2013; Vardopoulos, 2023). Results indicated a tendency toward (latent) settlement compaction within the study area (*e.g.*, Tomao *et al.*, 2022). The most rapid trend toward compaction is observed along the Greater Athens

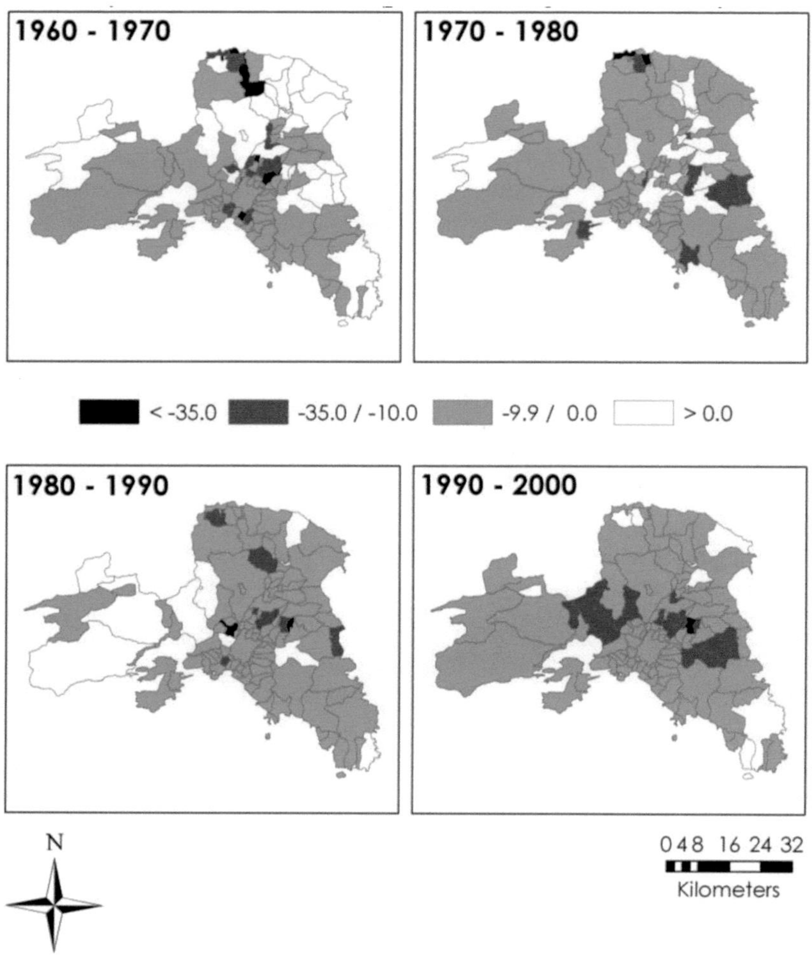

Figure 4.3 The progressive disappearance of cropland in metropolitan Athens mainly due to urbanization (percent change over time by decade). Source: Authors' own elaboration of publicly accessible data from the Hellenic Statistical Authority (ELSTAT).

fringe (*e.g.* Salvati, 2019), a district characterized by medium-compact and dense settlements developing radio-centrically over the past 50 years (see Vinci *et al.*, 2023). Peripheral areas, especially in Eastern Attica (Figure 4.3), still display a tendency toward dispersion, although the 2007 crisis (see Maris *et al.*, 2022) indirectly contained economic impulses toward sprawl (*e.g.*, Salvati, 2016). The most evident trend toward compaction was observed in demographically dynamic local contexts within distances less than 10 km from the city center (Morelli *et al.*, 2014). In municipalities with a town master plan officially adopted and mandated by legal regulations, trends toward compaction were more pronounced, particularly during economic expansion in the early 2000s (D'Agata *et al.*, 2023).

Suburban municipalities situated near the coast (see Economou and Mitoula, 2013), characterized by higher per-capita income, a substantial participation rate in the job market, and an elevated present-to-resident population ratio (see Salvati, 2016; Grigoriadis and Salvati, 2015), witness the most significant settlement dispersion. These contexts exhibit socioeconomic characteristics that encourage urban dispersion (Salvati, 2019). A diachronic perspective further underscores the significant role played by town master plans (Salvati and Zambon, 2017). Beyond any doubt, the number of detached buildings decreased in municipalities where a master plan was legally standing and binding. On the other hand, the present-to-resident population ratio emerged as a crucial variable associated with settlement dispersion (Tomao *et al.*, 2022). In alignment with the aforementioned findings, this analysis unequivocally emphasizes how marginalized contexts remain more susceptible to the socioeconomic forces driving settlement dispersion (Talen *et al.*, 2016).

Navigating the Quest for Sustainable Urban Forms: Challenges and Strategies for Effective Land-Use Policies in Contemporary Cities

According to Vallance *et al.* (2005), the quest for more sustainable urban forms has revitalized urban planning, with various types of urban infill and intensification gaining popularity among local authorities. The transformation of single-family home settlements is a central issue in the search for a more sustainable city. Local authorities are increasingly concerned with its associated impacts, even when they do not have clear planning strategies (Tammaru *et al.*, 2009).

Promoting self-contained expansion based on compaction and infill processes is a simplified strategy to control low-density urban dispersion and reduce land take (Pendall, 1999; Sorensen, 2000; Paul and Tonts, 2005; Halleux *et al.*, 2012). For instance, urban infill has been advocated as an economical use of existing infrastructure and a remedy for sprawl (Phan *et al.*, 2008; Shapurjee and Charlton, 2013; Sparshott *et al.*, 2018; Schwake, 2020; Vardopoulos, 2023). Infill, defined as the use of land within a built-up area for further construction, especially as part of a community redevelopment or growth management program, is a component of "smart

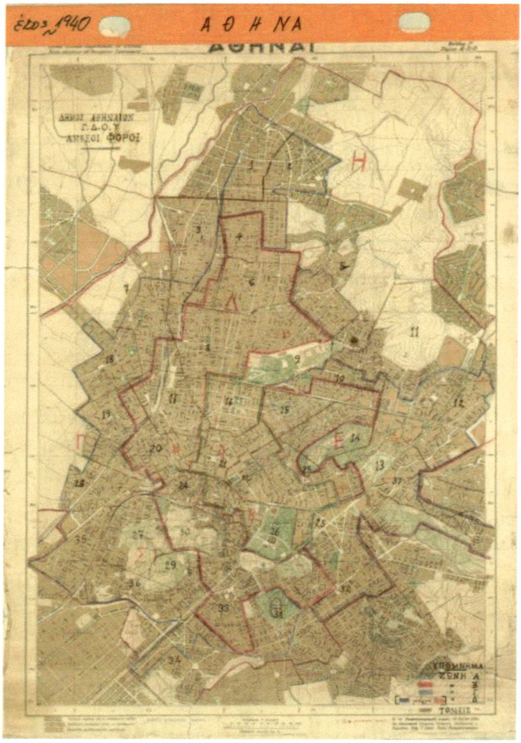

Figure 4.4 A pre-war zoning map of central Athens. Source: Authors' own elaboration and adaptation of public archive's maps.

growth" addressing unwanted side effects such as overloaded urban services (Figure 4.4), increased traffic congestion and pollution, and a decrease in green spaces (Kytta *et al.*, 2011; van Rensburg and Campbell, 2012; Abedini and Khalili, 2019; Holden, 2019; Papademetriou *et al.*, 2023).

All things considered, this study underscores the necessity for urban containment policies to continually adapt to evolving socioeconomic contexts and environmental/territorial constraints (Newton and Glackin, 2014; Leino *et al.*, 2018; Pettit *et al.*, 2018). This addresses the existing gap in truly effective practical solutions to urban containment challenges (Couch *et al.*, 2005; Masini *et al.*, 2019; Nickayin et al, 2020). Echoing the sentiments of Haase *et al.* (2013), one of the primary challenges facing cities and planners in the future is the development of new urbanization concepts that align with current household developments and changes/needs in housing forms/arrangements. This entails finding strategies to counteract the trend toward increasingly unsustainable land consumption (Salvia *et al.*, 2019).

These policies are increasingly required to align with the overarching objective of zero-net land consumption (Paul and Tonts, 2005; Gennaio *et al.*, 2009; Baing, 2010; Kim *et al.*, 2015). The efficacy of zero-net land consumption strategies, a key goal of the United Nations Sustainable Development program (Mindrinos and Panagiotopoulos, 2023), relies on the continuous monitoring of land consumption (Munafò *et al.*, 2013). The operational framework proposed in this study can inform policy strategies, providing a reference scenario for the integrated modeling of local-scale compaction vs. dispersion processes, forming the basis of the dominant urban model (Sevenant and Antrop, 2007; Marois and Bélanger, 2015; Ramachandra *et al.*, 2015).

In this context, the impact of spatial policies, specifically the enforcement of town master plans, on urban trends emphasizes the need for sustainable development strategies to more effectively align with evolving socioeconomic contexts (Weilenmann *et al.*, 2017). This entails defining "a set of specific rules that can limit the uncontrolled sprawl by contextualizing these general and widely accepted principles to local conditions" (La Greca *et al.*, 2011). It underscores the importance of spatial planning in regulating dispersed urban growth, even in social contexts where informal settlements had driven urban growth in earlier decades (Aguilar, 2008; Zhang *et al.*, 2011; Zhu and Guo, 2013).

Drawing from these findings, a sustainable development strategy oriented toward urban containment can derive benefits from place-based local development actions (Wu and Zhang, 2012) and a specific zoning based on the peculiarity of Mediterranean localities, and their intrinsic nexus with natural and cultural amenities (Vardopoulos *et al.*, 2023) (Figure 4.5). This approach should be integrated with a broader strategy that links regional developmental policies with socio-demographic measures aiming to regulate land prices.

Concluding Remarks

The intricate dynamics of metropolitan expansion and urbanization patterns underscore the pressing need for strategic and adaptive planning in the face of evolving socioeconomic contexts and environmental challenges (Salvati *et al.*, 2018). The juxtaposition of radio-centric growth and urban dispersion in advanced economies, particularly evident in Southern Europe, highlights the complex interplay between demographic forces, economic development, and planning regulations (Salvati, 2023; D'Agata *et al.*, 2023). This study advocates for a nuanced understanding of settlement compactness and dispersion, emphasizing the pivotal role of local contexts, municipal town

Figure 4.5 In-between compactness and dispersion: the intrinsic linkage between coastal cities and the Mediterranean Sea in the renewed waterfront of Eastern Barcelona, Spain. Source: Authors' photographic archive.

planning, and the intrinsic characteristics of marginalized areas in shaping these patterns.

The analysis of the Athens metropolitan region serves as a paradigmatic illustration of the challenges and opportunities inherent in navigating the quest for sustainable urban forms, shedding light on the multifaceted trends of settlement compaction and dispersion (see Vinci *et al.*, 2023). The observed tendencies, influenced by economic factors, town master plans, and geographical features, provide valuable insights for crafting effective strategies for sustainable urban development. As cities grapple with evolving socio-economic contexts and environmental constraints, this study underscores the importance of adopting a holistic approach, integrating place-based local development actions with broader regional policies, thus moving beyond traditional land-use analyses to consider the structural nuances of urban landscapes.

Furthermore, the quest for sustainable urban forms emerges as a central theme, driving the exploration of policies and development strategies geared toward urban containment and zero-net land consumption and beyond (Vardopoulos *et al.*, 2020). In essence, the findings emphasize the continuous adaptation of urban containment policies and the development of innovative urbanization concepts that align with evolving societal needs and environmental imperatives. This study stands as a valuable tool, providing insights and reference scenarios for policymakers and planners striving to foster more sustainable, resilient, and well-balanced urban landscapes.

References

Abedini, A., and Khalili, A. (2019). Determining the capacity infill development in growing metropolitans: A case study of Urmia city. Journal of Urban Management, 8(2), 316–327.

Aguilar, A.G. (2008). Peri-urbanization, illegal settlements and environmental impact in Mexico City. Cities, 25, 133–145.

Allen, A. (2003). Environmental planning and management of the peri-urban interface: perspectives on an emerging field. Environment and Urbanization, 15(1), 135–148.

Baing, A.S. (2010). Containing urban sprawl? Comparing brownfield reuse policies in England and Germany. International Planning Studies, 15(1), 25–35.

Bruegmann, R. (2005). Sprawl: a compact history. University of Chicago Press, Chicago.

Carlucci, M., Grigoriadis, E., Rontos, K., and Salvati, L. (2017). Revisiting an Hegemonic Concept: Long-term 'Mediterranean Urbanization' in between city re-polarization and metropolitan decline. Applied Spatial Analysis and Policy, 10(3), 347–362.

Ceccarelli, T., Bajocco, S., Perini, L., and Salvati, L. (2014). Urbanisation and Land Take of High Quality Agricultural Soils - Exploring Long-term Land Use Changes and Land Capability in Northern Italy. International Journal of Environmental Research, 8(1), 181–192.

Cheshire, P., and Magrini, S. (2009). Urban growth drivers in a Europe of sticky people and implicit boundaries. Journal of Economic Geography, 9 (1), 85–115.

Colantoni, A., Grigoriadis, E., Sateriano, A., Venanzoni, G., and Salvati, L. (2016). Cities as selective land predators? A Lesson on Urban Growth, (Un)effective planning and Sprawl Containment. Science of the Total Environment, 545-546, 329–339.

Colantoni, A., Mavrakis, A., Sorgi, T., and Salvati, L. (2015). Towards a 'polycentric' landscape? Reconnecting fragments into an integrated network of coastal forests in Rome. Rendiconti Accademia Nazionale dei Lincei, 26(3), 615–624.

Corona, P. (2018). Communicating facts, findings and thinking to support evidence-based strategies and decisions. Annals of Silvicultural Research, 42(1), 1–2.

Corona, P. (2019). Global change and silvicultural research. Annals of Silvicultural Research, 43(1), 1–3.

Couch, C., Karecha, J., Nuissl, H., and Rink, D. (2005). Decline and sprawl: an evolving type of urban development – Observed in Liverpool and Leipzig. European Planning Studies, 13(1), 117–136.

Couch, C., Petschel-held, G., and Leontidou, L., (2007). Urban Sprawl In Europe: Landscapes, Land-use Change and Policy. Blackwell, London.

Cuadrado-Ciuraneta, S., Durà-Guimerà, A., and Salvati, L. (2017). Not only tourism: unravelling suburbanization, second-home expansion and "rural" sprawl in Catalonia, Spain. Urban Geography, 38(1), 66–89.

D'Agata, A., Alaimo, L. S., Cudlín, P., and Salvati, L. (2023). Easy come, easy go: Short-term land-use dynamics vis à vis regional economic downturns. Socio-Economic Planning Sciences, 88, 101603.

D'Agata, A., Ciaschini, C., Mosconi, E. M., Rodrigo-Comino, J., Vardopoulos, I., Scarpitta, D., Alhuseen, A. M. A., and Salvati, L. (2024). The latent shift from monocentric to polycentric settlement models. In A. Sateriano (Ed.), Urban Crisis: Social and Economic Implications for Southern Europe. Nova Science: Hauppauge, NY, USA. ISBN: 979-8-89113-242-9.

D'Agata, A., Nosova, B., Vardopoulos, I., Rontos, K., Clemente, M., Colombo, C., Sateriano, A., and Salvati, L. (2024). Urban decline, Economic crisis and fringe landscapes: The Mediterranean experience. In A. Sateriano (Ed.), Urban Crisis: Social and Economic Implications for Southern Europe. Nova Science: Hauppauge, NY, USA. ISBN: 979-8-89113-242-9.

D'Agata, A., Ponza, D., Strolu, F. A., Vardopoulos, I., Rontos, K., Escrivà, F., Chelli, F., Alaimo, L. S., Luca, S., and Nickayin, S. S. (2023). Toward sustainable development trajectories? Estimating urban footprints from high-resolution copernicus layers in Athens, Greece. Land, 12(8), 1490.

Di Feliciantonio, C., and Salvati, L. (2015). 'Southern' Alternatives of Urban Diffusion: Investigating Settlement Characteristics and Socio-Economic Patterns in Three Mediterranean Regions. Tijdschrift Voor Economische En Sociale Geografie, 106(4), 453–470.

Di Feliciantonio, C., and Salvati, L. (2015). 'Southern' Alternatives of Urban Diffusion: Investigating Settlement Characteristics and Socio-Economic

Patterns in Three Mediterranean Regions. Tijdschrift voor Economische en Sociale Geografie, 106(4), 453–470.

Di Feliciantonio, C., Salvati, L., Sarantakou, E., and Rontos, K. (2018). Class diversification, economic growth and urban sprawl: Evidences from a pre-crisis European city. Quality & Quantity, 52(4), 1501–1522.

Doukas, Y. E., Maravegias, N., and Andreou, G. (Eds.). (2022). Η χωρική διάσταση της ευρωπαϊκής ολοκλήρωσης: σύγκλιση ή απόκλιση; Dionicos: Athens, Greece. ISBN: 978-6185-6650-3-6.

Duvernoy, I., Zambon, I., Sateriano, A., and Salvati, L. (2018). Pictures from the Other Side of the Fringe: Urban Growth and Peri-urban Agriculture in a Post-industrial City (Toulouse, France). Journal of Rural Studies, 57, 25–35.

Economou, A., and Mitoula, R. (2013). Management of natural resources and protection of the coastal urban area of Glyfada. Land Use Policy, 35, 204–212.

European Environment Agency (2006). Urban sprawl in Europe – The ignored challenge. EEA Report 10, Copenhagen.

Forster, C. (2006). The Challenge of Change: Australian Cities and Urban Planning in the New Millennium. Geographical Research, 44(2), 173–182.

Frenkel, A. (2004). The potential effect of national growth-management policy on urban sprawl and the depletion of open spaces and farmland. Land Use Policy, 21, 357–369.

Gennaio, M.-P., Hersperger, A.M., and Burgi, M. (2009). Containing urban sprawl—Evaluating effectiveness of urban growth boundaries set by the Swiss Land Use Plan. Land Use Policy, 26, 224–232.

Giannakourou, G. (2005). Transforming spatial planning policy in the Mediterranean countries. European Planning Studies, 13(2), 319–331.

Gil, M.T.N., Carvalho, L., and Paiva, I. (2020). Determining factors in becoming a sustainable smart city: An empirical study in Europe. Economics & Sociology, 13(1), 24–39.

Grekousis, G., Manetos, P., and Photis, Y.N. (2013). Modeling urban evolution using neural networks, fuzzy logic and GIS: The case of the Athens metropolitan area. Cities, 30, 193–203.

Grigoriadis, E., and Salvati, L. (2015). Recession in Action: Exploring the Spatial Divergence of Per capita Income in Greece. Romanian Journal of Regional Science, 2, 9(2), 68–83.

Haase, D., Kabisch, N., and Haase, A. (2013). Endless urban growth? On the mismatch of population, household and urban land area growth and its effects on the urban debate. PLoS One, 8(6).

Halleux, J.M., Marcinczak, S., and van der Krabben, E. (2012). The adaptive efficiency of land use planning measured by the control of urban sprawl. The cases of the Netherlands, Belgium and Poland. Land Use Policy, 29(4), 887–898.

Hasse, J.E., and Lathrop, R.G. (2003). Land resource impact indicators of urban sprawl. Applied Geography, 23, 159–175.

Heim, C.E. (2001). Leapfrogging, Urban Sprawl, and Growth Management: Phoenix, 1950–2000. American Journal of Economics and Sociology, 60(1), 245–283.

Hewitt, R., and Escobar, F. (2011). The territorial dynamics of fast-growing regions: Unsustainable land use change and future policy challenges in Madrid, Spain. Applied Geography, 31(2), 650–667.

Holden, M. (2019). Bringing the neighbourhood into urban infill development in the interest of well-being. International Journal of Community Well-being, 1(2), 137–155.

Hongling, Y.I.N., and Teng, X.U. (2013). The mismatch between population urbanization and land urbanization in China. In Urban Planning Forum, 2(217), 10–15.

Hoymann, J. (2011). Accelerating urban sprawl in depopulating regions: a scenario analysis for the Elbe River Basin. Regional Environmental Change, 11, 73–86.

Jabareen, Y.R. (2006). Sustainable Urban Forms. Their Typologies, Models, and Concepts. Journal of Planning Education and Research, 26(1), 38–52.

Jaeger, J.A.G., Bertiller, R., Schwick, C., Cavens, D., and Kienast, F. (2010). Urban permeation of landscapes and sprawl per capita: New measures of urban sprawl. Ecological Indicators, 10(2), 427–441.

Kazemzadeh-Zow, A., Zanganeh Shahraki, S., Salvati, L., and Samani, N.N. (2017). A spatial zoning approach to calibrate and validate urban growth models. International Journal of Geographical Information Science, 31(4), 763–782.

Kim, J.H., Cho, J., and Keane, T.D. (2015). Political fragmentation and land use changes in the Interior Plains. Population and Environment, 37(1), 63–82.

Kyttä, M., Kahila, M., and Broberg, A. (2011). Perceived environmental quality as an input to urban infill policy-making. Urban Design International, 16(1), 19–35.

La Greca, P., Barbarossa, L., Ignaccolo, M., Inturri, G., and Martinico, F. (2011). The density dilemma. A proposal for introducing smart growth principles in a sprawling settlement within Catania Metropolitan Area. Cities, 28(6), 527–535.

Lambin, E.F., and Meyfroidt, P. (2010). Land use transitions: Socio-ecological feedback versus socio-economic change. Land Use Policy, 27(2), 108–118.

Lauf, S., Haase, D., and Kleinschmit, B. (2016). The effects of growth, shrinkage, population aging and preference shifts on urban development—A spatial scenario analysis of Berlin, Germany. Land Use Policy, 52, 240–254.

Leino, H., Santaoja, M., and Laine, M. (2018). Researchers as knowledge brokers: translating knowledge or co-producing legitimacy? An urban infill case from Finland. International Planning Studies, 23(2), 119–129.

Lemonakis, C., Alexopoulos, G., Garefalakis, A., and Garefalakis, S. (2024). Trends and new elements in urban hierarchy research: the Greek paradigm. The Annals of Regional Science, 72, 335–354.

Maravegias, N., and Doukas, Y. E. (2012). A stategy for rural development in Greece: The case of Island Areas. Region & Periphery, 1, 37–56.

Maris, G., Sklias, P., and Maravegias, N. (2022). The political economy of the Greek economic crisis in 2020. European Politics and Society, 23(4), 447–467.

Marois, G., and Bélanger, A. (2015). Analyzing the impact of urban planning on population distribution in the Montreal metropolitan area using a small-area microsimulation projection model. Population and Environment, 37(2), 131–156.

Martinuzzi, S., Gould, W.A., and Ramos Gonzalez, O.M. (2007). Land development, land use, and urban sprawl in Puerto Rico integrating remote sensing and population census data. Landscape and Urban Planning, 79, 288–297.

Mitoula, R., and Papavasileiou, A. (2023). Mega infrastructure projects and their contribution to sustainable development: the case of the Athens Metro. Economic Change and Restructuring, 56(3), 1943–1969.

Morelli, V.G., Rontos, K., and Salvati, L. (2014). Between suburbanisation and re-urbanisation: Revisiting the urban life cycle in a Mediterranean compact city. Urban Research & Practice, 7(1), 74–88.

Munafò, M., Salvati, L., and Zitti, M. (2013). Estimating soil sealing at country scale – Italy as a case study. Ecological Indicators, 26, 36–43.

Newton, P., and Glackin, S. (2014). Understanding infill: Towards new policy and practice for urban regeneration in the established suburbs of Australia's cities. Urban Policy and Research, 32(2), 121–143.

Nickayin, S. S., Tomao, A., Quaranta, G., Salvati, L., and Gimenez Morera, A. (2020). Going toward Resilience? Town Planning, Peri-Urban Landscapes, and the Expansion of Athens, Greece. Sustainability, 12(24), 10471.

Ningal, T., Hartemink, A.E., and Bregt, A.K. (2008). Land use change and population growth in the Morobe Province of Papua New Guinea between 1975 and 2000. Journal of Environmental Management, 87(1), 117–124.

Orenstein, D.E., and Hamburg, S.P. (2010). Population and pavement: population growth and land development in Israel. Population and Environment, 31(4), 223–254.

Oueslati, W., Alvanides, S., and Garrod, G. (2015). Determinants of urban sprawl in European cities. Urban Studies, 52(9), 1594–1614.

Panagiotopoulos, P., and Mendrinos, L. (2023). Measuring sustainable development: A weighting approach to sustainable development indicators. International Journal of Multidisciplinary Research and Analysis, 6(9), 4510–4520.

Panori, A., Psycharis, Y., and Ballas, D. (2019). Spatial segregation and migration in the city of Athens: Investigating the evolution of urban socio-spatial immigrant structures. Population, Space and Place, 25(5), e2209.

Papademetriou, C., Ragazou, K., Garefalakis, A., and Passas, I. (2023). Green Human Resource Management: Mapping the Research Trends for Sustainable and Agile Human Resources in SMEs. Sustainability, 15(7), 5636.

Paul, V., and Tonts, M. (2005). Containing urban sprawl: trends in land use and spatial planning in the Metropolitan Region of Barcelona. Journal of Environmental Planning and Management, 48(1), 7–35.

Paulsen, K. (2013). Geography, policy or market? New evidence on the measurement and causes of sprawl (and infill) in US metropolitan regions. Urban Studies, 51(12), 2629–2645.

Pendall, R. (1999). Do land-use controls cause sprawl? Environment and Planning B: Planning and Design, 26(4), 555–571.

Pettit, C., Bakelmun, A., Lieske, S.N., Glackin, S., Thomson, G., Shearer, H., and Newman, P. (2018). Planning support systems for smart cities. City, Culture and Society, 12, 13–24.

Phan, T., Peterson, J., and Chandra, S. (2008). Urban infill: extent and implications in the City of Monash. People and Place, 16(4), 23–31.

Pili, S., Grigoriadis, E., Carlucci, M., Clemente, M., and Salvati, L. (2017). Towards Sustainable Growth? A Multi-criteria Assessment of (Changing) Urban Forms. Ecological Indicators, 76, 71–80.

Ragazou, K., Passas, I., Garefalakis, A., Kourgiantakis, M., and Xanthos, G. (2022). Youth's Entrepreneurial Intention: A Multinomial Logistic Regression Analysis of the Factors Influencing Greek HEI Students in Time of Crisis. Sustainability, 14(20), 13164.

Rahimi, A. (2016). A methodological approach to urban land-use change modeling using infill development pattern—a case study in Tabriz, Iran. Ecological Processes, 5(1), 1–15.

Ramachandra, T.V., Bharath, A.H., and Sowmyashree, M.V. (2015). Monitoring urbanization and its implications in a mega city from space: Spatiotemporal patterns and its indicators. Journal of Environmental Management, 148, 67–81.

Rontos, K., Grigoriadis, S., Sateriano, A., Syrmali, M., Vavouras, I., and Salvati, L. 2016. Lost in Protest, Found in Segregation: Divided Cities in the Light of the 2015 'Oki' Referendum in Greece. City, Culture and Society, 7(3), 139–148.

Salvati, L. (2016). The Dark Side of the Crisis: Disparities in per Capita income (2000–12) and the Urban-Rural Gradient in Greece. Tijdschrift voor Economische en Sociale Geografie, 107(5), 628–641.

Salvati, L. (2016). The Dark Side of the Crisis: Disparities in per Capita income (2000-12) and the Urban-Rural Gradient in Greece. Tijdschrift Voor Economische En Sociale Geografie, 107(5), 628–641.

Salvati, L. (2019). Urban dispersion and economic crisis: empirical evidence from a Mediterranean region. Journal of Environmental Planning and Management, 62(7), 1205–1226.

Salvati, L. (2019). Urban dispersion and economic crisis: empirical evidence from a Mediterranean region. Journal of Environmental Planning and Management, 62(7), 1205–1226.

Salvati, L. (2023). Mono-centrism as a Destiny? An Econometric Test of Urban Models Using Building Activity. Applied Spatial Analysis and Policy, 16(1), 63–90.

Salvati, L., and Zambon, I. (2017). Social forces, urban growth, and town planning: Evolving visions from a contemporary metropolis. Current Politics & Economics of Europe, 28(2), 107–130.

Salvati, L., Carlucci, M., Grigoriadis, E., and Chelli, F. M. (2018). Uneven dispersion or adaptive polycentrism? Urban expansion, population dynamics and employment growth in an 'ordinary' city. Review of Regional Research, 38(1), 1–25.

Salvati, L., Ranalli, F., and Gitas, I. (2014). Landscape fragmentation and the agro-forest ecosystem along a rural-to-urban gradient: an exploratory study. International Journal of Sustainable Development & World Ecology, 21(2), 160–167.

Salvati, L., Sateriano, A., and Grigoriadis, E. (2016). Crisis and the city: Profiling urban growth under economic expansion and stagnation. Letters in Spatial and Resource Sciences, 9(3), 329–342.

Salvati, L., and Serra, P. (2016). Estimating rapidity of change in complex urban systems: a multidimensional, local-scale approach. Geographical Analysis, 48(2), 132–156.

Salvati, L., Zambon, I., Chelli, F. M., and Serra, P. (2018). Do spatial patterns of urbanization and land consumption reflect different socioeconomic contexts in Europe? Science of The Total Environment, 625, 722–730.

Salvati, L., Zitti, M., and Carlucci, M. (2017). In-between regional disparities and spatial heterogeneity: a multivariate analysis of territorial divides in Italy. Journal of Environmental Planning and Management, 60(6), 997–1015.

Schwake, G. (2020). The bourgeoisification of the Green-Line: The new Israeli middle-class and the Suburban Settlement. Political Geography, 82, 102223.

Sevenant, M., and Antrop, M. (2007). Settlement models, land use and visibility in rural landscapes: Two case studies in Greece. Landscape and urban planning, 80(4), 362–374.

Shapurjee, Y., and Charlton, S. (2013). Transforming South Africa's low-income housing projects through backyard dwellings: Intersections with households and the state in Alexandra, Johannesburg. Journal of Housing and the Built Environment, 28(4), 653–666.

Simon, D. (2008). Urban environments: issues on the peri-urban fringe. Annual Review of Environment and Resources, 33, 167–185.

Sorensen, A. (2000). Land readjustment and metropolitan growth: an examination of suburban land development and urban sprawl in the Tokyo metropolitan area. Progress in Planning, 53, 217–330.

Sparshott, P.J., Darchen, S., and Stjohn, D. (2018). Do sustainability rating tools deliver the best outcomes in master planned urban infill projects? City to the Lake experience. Australian Planner, 55(2), 84–92.

Talen, E., Anselin, L., Lee, S., and Koschinsky, J. (2016). Looking for logic: the zoning—land use mismatch. Landscape and Urban Planning, 152, 27–38.

Tammaru, T., Leetmaa, K., Silm, S., and Ahas, R. (2009). Temporal and spatial dynamics of the new residential areas around Tallinn. European Planning Studies, 17(3), 423–439.

Thinh, N.X., Arlt, G., Heber, B., Hennersdorf, J., and Lehmann, I. (2002). Evaluation of urban land-use structures with a view to sustainable development. Environmental Impact Assessment Review, 22(5), 475–492.

Turok, I., and Mykhnenko, V., (2007). The trajectories of European cities, 1960-2005. Cities 24(3), 165–182.

Vallance, S., Perkins, H.C., and Moore, K. (2005). The results of making a city more compact: neighbours' interpretation of urban infill. Environment and Planning B: Planning and Design, 32(5), 715–733.

van Rensburg, J.D.J., and Campbell, M.M. (2012). The Management of Urban Sprawl by Applying an Urban Edge Strategy. Urban Forum, 23(1), 61–72.

Vardopoulos, I. (2023). Adaptive reuse for sustainable development and land use: A multivariate linear regression analysis estimating key determinants of public perceptions. Heritage, 6(2), 809–828.

Vardopoulos, I., and Theodoropoulou, E. (2018). Does the new 'FIX' fit? Adaptive building reuse affecting local sustainable development: preliminary results. In Urban Heritage and the Modern City. The International Academic Forum (IAFOR) Conference on Heritage and the City (HCNY2018), 7-9 November 2018. New York, USA. Official Conference Proceedings (pp. 97–114). International Academic Forum (IAFOR): Naka Ward, Nagoya, Aichi Japan. ISSN: 2434-5903

Vardopoulos, I., Giannopoulos, K., Papaefthymiou, E., Temponera, E., Chatzithanasis, G., Goussia-Rizou, M., Karymbalis, E., Michalakelis, C., Tsartas, P., and Sdrali, D. (2023). Urban buildings sustainable adaptive reuse into tourism accommodation establishments: a SOAR analysis. Discover Sustainabiity, 4(1), 50.

Vardopoulos, I., Ioannides, S., Georgiou, M., Voukkali, I., Salvati, L., and Doukas, Y. E. (2023). Shaping sustainable cities: A long-rerm GIS-emanated spatial analysis of settlement growth and planning in a coastal Mediterranean European city. Sustainability, 15(14), 11202.

Vardopoulos, I., Papoui-Evangelou, M., Nosovo, B., and Salvati, L. (2023). Smart 'tourist cities' revisited: culture-led urban sustainability and the global real estate market. Sustainability, 15(5), 4313.

Vinci, S., Vardopoulos, I., and Salvati, L. (2023). A tale of a shrinking City? Exploring the complex interplay of socio-demographic dynamics in the recent development of Attica, Greece. Cities, 132, 104089.

Vittorio Gargiulo, M., and Salvati, L. (2010). Ad Hoc Urban Sprawl in the Mediterranean City: Dispersing a Compact Tradition? Edizioni Nuova Cultura: Rome Italy. ISBN: 9788861345720.

Weilenmann, B., Seidl, I., and Schulz, T. (2017). The socio-economic determinants of urban sprawl between 1980 and 2010 in Switzerland. Landscape and Urban Planning, 157, 468-482.

Wilson, C.R., and Brown, D.G. (2015). Change in visible impervious surface area in southeastern Michigan before and after the "Great Recession:" spatial differentiation in remotely sensed land-cover dynamics. Population and Environment, 36(3), 331–355.

Wissen Hayek, U., Jaeger, J.A.G., Schwick, C., Jarne, A., and Schuler, M. (2011). Measuring and Assessing Urban Sprawl: What are the Remaining Options for Future Settlement Development in Switzerland for 2030? Applied Spatial Analysis and Policy, 4(4), 249–279.

Wu, K., and Zhang, H. (2012). Land use dynamics, built-up land expansion patterns, and driving forces analysis of the fast-growing Hangzhou metropolitan area, eastern China (1978–2008). Applied Geography, 34, 137–145.

Zambon, I., Benedetti, A., Ferrara, C., and Salvati, L. (2018). Soil Matters? A Multivariate Analysis of Socioeconomic Constraints to Urban Expansion in Mediterranean Europe. Ecological Economics, 146, 173–183.

Zambon, I., Serra, P., Sauri, D., Carlucci, M., and Salvati, L. (2017). Beyond the 'Mediterranean City': Socioeconomic Disparities and Urban Sprawl in three Southern European Cities. Geographiska Annaler, B 99(3), 319–337.

Zhang, T. (2001). Community features and urban sprawl: the case of the Chicago metropolitan region. Land Use Policy, 18, 221–232.

Zhang, X., Wu, Y., and Shen, L. (2011). An evaluation framework for the sustainability of urban land use: A study of capital cities and municipalities in China. Habitat International, 35, 141–149.

Zhu, J., and Guo, Y. (2013). Fragmented Peri-urbanisation Led by Autonomous Village Development under Informal Institution in High-density Regions: The Case of Nanhai, China. Urban Studies, 51(6), 1120–1145.

5

From “Cityscape” to “Poolside”: A Comprehensive Analysis of Sprawl in the Mediterranean

Ioannis Vardopoulos, Adele Sateriano, Luca Salvati, and Francisco Escrivà Saneugenio

Urban growth encompasses a multifaceted set of characteristics that have been extensively explored by scholars (Musterd and Ostendorf, 1998; Kazepov, 2005; Cassier and Kesteloot, 2012; Vardopoulos *et al.*, 2023 Doukas, 2011). This intricate phenomenon involves the dynamic interplay of various social, economic, and environmental factors, giving rise to distinct patterns and morphologies within urban areas (Hatzi, 2010; Vardopoulos *et al.*, 2023; Lemonakis et al, 2023).

A contemporary manifestation of urban development is the concept of urban sprawl, a model with far-reaching implications across social, economic, and environmental domains (Burchell *et al.*, 1998; Brueckner, 2000; Galster *et al.*, 2001; Frenkel and Ashkenazi, 2008; Orenstein *et al.*, 2013). Urban sprawl is characterized by the expansion of low-density settlements, often replacing agricultural lands and forests (Salvati *et al.*, 2012; Surya *et al.*, 2021; D’Agata *et al.*, 2023). The resulting landscape is a mosaic dominated by detached houses (Figure 5.1), reflecting a shift away from traditional urban forms (Salvati *et al.*, 2015; D’Agata *et al.*, 2024). One noteworthy aspect of sprawl is its reliance on private transportation (Burchell *et al.*, 1998; Tsai, 2005; Torrens, 2008). As sprawling developments take shape, there is a discernible shift in transportation patterns, with residents depending significantly on private vehicles (Cao *et al.*,2007). This shift not only impacts the daily lives of the residents but also has broader implications for the environment (Colvile *et al.*, 2001; Vardopoulos, 2019), contributing to issues such as increased carbon emissions and traffic congestion (Lu *et al.*, 2021).

The encroachment of low-density settlements into cropland and forests raises critical questions about sustainability and land-use planning

Figure 5.1 The compact Mediterranean city: the stratification of shapes and forms in downtown Monopoli, Apulia, in Southern Italy.

(Theobald, 2001; Bren d'Amour *et al.*, 2016; Cui *et al.*, 2019). The transformation of natural landscapes into a mixed urban fabric underscores the complex interplay between human settlements and the environment (Piña and Martínez, 2014; Rees and Wackernagel, 1996). Understanding the nuances of urban sprawl is vital for devising effective policies that balance the need for development with environmental preservation and sustainable urban living (Ahani and Dadashpoor, 2021; Tombolini *et al.*, 2022; Doukas *et al.*, 2023). The exploration of urban growth and sprawl involves a rich tapestry of factors that shape the evolving landscape of human habitation (Hatzi, 2010; Glaeser and Kahn, 2004; Vardopoulos *et al.*, 2020). Drawing on the insights of various scholars enables a holistic understanding of these phenomena, paving the way for informed decision-making in the realms of urban planning, environmental conservation, and social development (Figure 5.2).

Mediterranean Mosaics: Tracing the Unique Paths of European Cities

Sprawl processes have undoubtedly generated economic advantages (Brueckner, 2001; Zambon *et al.*, 2017), but they come at a considerable cost to the environment and society (Gallagher, 2001; Escolano *et al.*, 2018), presenting a formidable challenge for sustainable land management and

Figure 5.2 Urban dispersion at the vineyards' fringe of medium-sized cities: Bozen, Northern Italy.

regional planning (Hasse and Lathrop, 2003; Kempton *et al.*, 2022). One critical impediment to a comprehensive understanding of sprawl patterns is the scarcity of high-resolution spatial data (Sudhira *et al.*, 2004; Ji *et al.*, 2006; D'Agata *et al.*, 2023), particularly in emerging countries and certain affluent regions (Frenkel and Ashkenazi, 2008; Doukas *et al.*, 2022). The absence of such data hampers the nuanced analysis required to unravel the complexity of sprawling developments (Welch, 1982).

In addition, this limitation in data availability underscores the importance of cross-country databases that house pertinent information at a granular, local scale (Wardrop, 2018; D'Agata *et al.*, 2023). These databases facilitate international comparisons, aiding in the identification of sprawl typologies across diverse socioeconomic contexts (D'Agata *et al.*, 2023). Recognizing the need for such cross-country data initiatives (Vermeiren *et al.*, 2022), the European Commission has spearheaded efforts to monitor urban expansion, yielding valuable outputs like the Urban Atlas (UA) initiative (Salvati *et al.*, 2013). The UA program has been instrumental in producing high-resolution land-use maps spanning nearly 300 urban areas from 2008 to 2010 (Montero *et al.*, 2014). However, the ongoing challenge lies in the sustainability of these initiatives, particularly in the context of remote-sensing data (Bhatta *et al.*, 2010; Shao *et al.*, 2020). Updating and adapting such data to the unique characteristics of different local contexts requires substantial financial resources (Franci *et al.*, 2015). Hence, the financial dimension becomes a pivotal factor

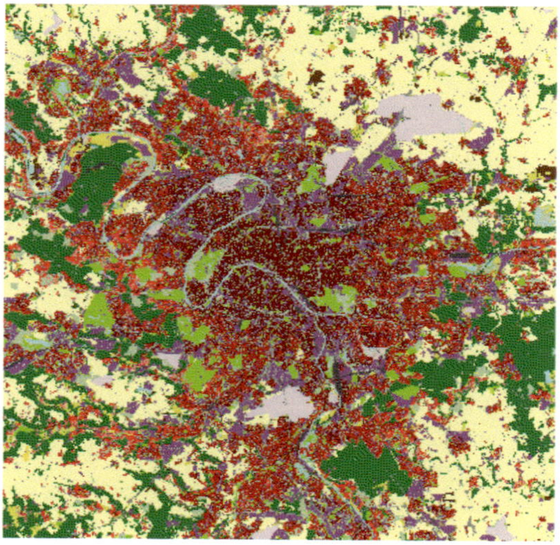

Figure 5.3 Paris' compact core and the surrounding sprawl seen from the European Urban Atlas initiative. Source: Authors' own adaptation of a free map archive of European Environment Agency.

in the continuous examination of urban growth and sprawl patterns in Europe (Hennig *et al.*, 2015).

While initiatives like the UA have made significant strides in providing valuable insights into urban expansion (Figure 5.3), the sustainable continuation of such efforts necessitates ongoing financial commitment and technical expertise (Tomko *et al.*, 2011; Keith and Parnell, 2023). Overcoming these challenges is imperative for fostering a comprehensive understanding of sprawl patterns, enabling informed decision-making in the realms of urban planning and sustainable land management (Salvati and Carlucci, 2016; Vardopoulos, 2023).

In the European context, the diversity among homogeneous groups of cities is striking, each characterized by specific forms and functions (Pisarevsakaya *et al.*, 2021; Salvati and Carlucci, 2015). Take, for example, Mediterranean cities, which exhibit distinctive morphologies shaped by a rich tapestry of economic, demographic, political, and cultural factors over their long-term history (King *et al.*, 1997; Vardopoulos *et al.*, 2023; Vinci *et al.*, 2023). The evolution of these cities reflects a complex interplay of influences, creating unique urban landscapes (Salvati, 2015).

Historically, Mediterranean cities experienced a predominantly deregulated and compact expansion during the 1960s and 1970s (Catalán *et al.*, 2008; Chorianopoulos *et al.*, 2010). However, a noteworthy shift has occurred in recent times, marked by a rapid transition toward a more dispersed morphology, as observed in Southern European cities (Schneider and Woodcock, 2008; Salvati *et al.*, 2013). This transition sets them apart from their Northern and Western European counterparts while sharing certain characteristics with non-European Mediterranean urban areas (Salvati and Gargiulo Morelli, 2014).

This nuanced evolution poses a challenge to the pan-European assessment of sprawl dynamics (Salvati and Carlucci, 2016). The distinctive patterns emerging in Southern European cities, contrasting with those in the north and west, contribute to a landscape that is not easily generalized (Salvati *et al.*, 2013). The complexities inherent in these variations make it imperative to approach the assessment of sprawl dynamics with a nuanced understanding, recognizing the multifaceted nature of urban development across different regions of Europe (Smiraglia *et al.*, 2021).

The diversity in the forms and functions of European cities, particularly exemplified by the distinctive evolution of Mediterranean cities, underscores the need for a careful and context-specific analysis of sprawl dynamics (Salvati and Gargiulo Morelli, 2014). Acknowledging the unique historical trajectories and influences shaping each urban landscape is essential for a comprehensive understanding of the complex patterns of urban growth and sprawl in Europe (Patacchini and Yenou, 2009; Hatzi, 2010; Salvati, 2018).

Swimming Pools as "Sprawl Barometers" in Mediterranean Urbanities

In the context of Mediterranean urban areas, there is a pressing need for effective indicators that can accurately assess sprawl patterns over time (Salvati *et al.*, 2015; Salvati *et al.*, 2013). The selection of sprawl indicators should adhere to fundamental criteria, as outlined by Jaeger *et al.* (2010). These criteria include ease of computation, graphical representation, flexibility, affordability, and comprehensibility to non-technical stakeholders (Jaeger *et al.*, 2010; Hasse and Lathrop, 2003).

Recognizing these criteria, the present study proposes and validates two indicators derived from the spatial distribution of residential swimming pools (Figure 5.4). These indicators are positioned as reliable proxies for capturing the nuances of sprawl in Mediterranean urban landscapes. The choice of swimming pools as indicators is rooted in their status as typical architectural elements within de-localized sprawl landscapes (Salvati *et al.*, 2014; Zambon *et al.*, 2015). These landscapes are characterized by settlements that are physically decoupled from core cities, transcending the traditional urban–rural dichotomy (Vidal *et al.*, 2011).

Figure 5.4 The evocative shape of a residential (peri-urban) landscape dominated by swimming pools and private gardens around villas.

The use of swimming pools as indicators aligns with the outlined criteria for effective sprawl assessment (Rodríguez-Cuenca and Alonso, 2014). First and foremost, their spatial distribution provides a tangible and easily computable metric (Carlucci *et al.*, 2020). Additionally, the graphical representation of swimming pool data offers a visual tool for stakeholders to grasp the extent of sprawl (Salvati *et al.*, 2016). The flexibility of these indicators ensures applicability across diverse Mediterranean urban contexts (Zambon *et al.*, 2017). Moreover, the relatively low cost associated with collecting and analyzing swimming pool data enhances the affordability of this approach (Salvati *et al.*, 2015). Crucially, the comprehensibility of the indicators to non-technical stakeholders makes them valuable tools for facilitating inclusive discussions and decision-making processes related to urban development (Zambon *et al.*, 2015).

The introduction and validation of these swimming-pool-derived indicators offer a promising avenue for comprehensively assessing sprawl patterns in Mediterranean urban areas (Zambon and Salvati, 2018). By meeting the

Figure 5.5 Urban sprawl and swimming pools in the United States.

criteria of easy computation, graphical representation, flexibility, cost-effectiveness, and accessibility to diverse stakeholders, these indicators contribute valuable insights into the evolving nature of urban landscapes in the region (Ridolfi *et al.*, 2017). As posited by Frenkel and Ashkenazi (2008), the multifaceted nature of sprawl necessitates quantification through distinct measures and observation over a sufficiently extended period. In this context, this study introduces swimming pools as relevant landmarks for peri-urban landscapes characterized by low- and medium-density settlements. Examining pool distribution serves to underscore the polarization between scattered low-density and compact high-density settlements, indicating the efficacy of the proposed indicators in identifying sprawl patterns.

Specifically, indicators can demonstrate their utility in identifying very-low density, isolated settlements (pools per population), and medium–low, discontinuous urban settlements (pools per area). This article positions pool indicators as commendable tools for monitoring sprawl on both local and regional scales due to their low-cost nature and comprehensiveness. Deriving these indicators from freely available sources, such as Google Earth diachronic imagery, ensures global spatial coverage and comparability across countries.

Crucially, this study validates the reliability and coherence of pool indicators over time, affirming their ability to discriminate between different sprawl patterns. The analysis not only highlights the effectiveness of these indicators in capturing the dynamics of sprawl but also emphasizes their potential for broader applicability in diverse geographical contexts. Overall, swimming pool indicators emerge as a practical, cost-effective, and globally applicable tool for monitoring and understanding sprawl, offering valuable insights for both local and regional planning efforts.

Concluding Remarks

The negative environmental consequences of urban sprawl emphasize the urgency for new strategies to address the escalating problem of land consumption in peri-urban areas. Meeting this challenge requires the development of reliable, homogeneous, and low-cost quantitative measurements, as underscored by Jaeger and Schwick (2014). In this context, pool indicators emerge as effective tools for assessing land consumption and can be easily disseminated to stakeholders with an interest in urban development. Beyond their utility in gauging land consumption, pool indicators offer a valuable means of assessing the impact of sprawl on natural resources, particularly in terms of water consumption. This expands the scope of these indicators, positioning them as versatile tools for understanding the broader environmental implications of urban expansion.

The applicability of pool indicators extends to emerging and economically disadvantaged countries, where technological facilities and spatial data availability may be limited. The simplicity and low-cost nature of these indicators make them accessible and adaptable, offering a means of monitoring sprawl patterns even in regions with constrained resources. Future research endeavors should prioritize the identification of socioeconomic and territorial profiles associated with varying pool densities. This deeper analysis can enhance our understanding of the complex interplay between urban development and its socioeconomic context. Additionally, the scope of the analysis can be broadened by creating diachronic maps on local, regional, and country levels. Integrating pool indicators with other relevant information will further enrich the monitoring of urban regions, providing a comprehensive understanding of the dynamics of sprawl over time.

In conclusion, the adoption of pool indicators not only addresses the immediate need for quantitative measurements in mitigating urban sprawl but also opens avenues for more extensive research and analysis. Their adaptability, simplicity, and cost-effectiveness make pool indicators valuable tools for comprehensively monitoring and addressing the environmental challenges posed by urban expansion in peri-urban areas, both locally and globally.

References

Alfonso Piña, W. H., and Pardo Martínez, C. I. (2014). Urban material flow analysis: An approach for Bogotá, Colombia. Ecological Indicators, 42, 32–42.

Bhatta, B., Saraswati, S., and Bandyopadhyay, D. (2010). Urban sprawl measurement from remote sensing data. Applied Geography, 30(4), 731–740.

Bren d'Amour, C., Reitsma, F., Baiocchi, G., Barthel, S., Güneralp, B., Erb, K.-H., Haberl, H., Creutzig, F., and Seto, K. C. (2017). Future urban land expansion and implications for global croplands. Proceedings of the National Academy of Sciences, 114(34), 8939–8944.

Brueckner, J. K. (2000). Urban sprawl: diagnosis and remedies. International Regional Science Review, 23(2), 160–171.

Brueckner, J. K., Mills, E., and Kremer, M. (2001). Urban Sprawl: Lessons from Urban Economics [with Comments]. Brookings-Wharton Papers on Urban Affairs, 65–97.

Burchell, R. W., Shad, N. A., Listokin, D., Phillips, H., Downs, A., Seskin, S., Davis, J., Moore, T., Helton, D. and Gall, M. (1998). The cost of sprawl-revisited. Transit Cooperative Research Program (TCRP). Report 39, Transportation Research Board, National Research Council, Washington, DC, 83–125

Carlucci, M., Vinci, S., Ricciardo Lamonica, G., and Salvati, L. (2022). Socio-spatial Disparities and the Crisis: Swimming Pools as a Proxy of Class Segregation in Athens. Social Indicators Research, 161(2–3), 937–961.

Cassiers, T. and Kesteloot, C. (2012). Socio-spatial Inequalities and Social Cohesion in European Cities. Urban Studies, 49(9), 1909–1924.

Catalán, B., Sauri, D. and Serra, P. (2008). Urban sprawl in the Mediterranean? Patterns of growth and change in the Barcelona Metropolitan Region 1993–2000. Landscape and Urban Planning, 85(3–4), 174–184.

Chorianopoulos, I., Pagonis, T., Koukoulas, S. and Drymoniti, S. (2010). Planning, competitiveness and sprawl in the Mediterranean city: The case of Athens. Cities, 27(4), 249–259.

Colvile, R., Hutchinson, E., Mindell, J., and Warren, R. (2001). The transport sector as a source of air pollution. Atmospheric Environment, 35(9), 1537–1565.

Couch, C., Petschel-Held, G. and Leontidou, L. (2007). Urban sprawl in Europe: landscapes, land-use change and policy. Oxford: Blackwell.

Cui, Y., Liu, J., Xu, X., Dong, J., Li, N., Fu, Y., Lu, S., Xia, H., Si, B., and Xiao, X. (2019). Accelerating Cities in an Unsustainable Landscape: Urban Expansion and Cropland Occupation in China, 1990–2030. Sustainability, 11(8), 2283.

D'Agata, A., Nosova, B., Vardopoulos, I., Rontos, K., Clemente, M., Colombo, C., Sateriano, A., and Salvati, L. (2024). Urban decline, Economic crisis and fringe landscapes: The Mediterranean experience. In A. Sateriano (Ed.), Urban Crisis: Social and Economic Implications for Southern Europe. Nova Science: Hauppauge, NY, USA. ISBN: 979-8-89113-242-9.

D'Agata, A., Ponza, D., Stroiu, F. A., Vardopoulos, I., Rontos, K., Escrivà, F., Chelli, F., Alaimo, L. S., Salvati, L., and Nickyain, S. S. (2023). Toward sustainable development trajectories? Estimating urban footprints from high-resolution copernicus layers in Athens, Greece. Land, 12(8), 1490.

Doukas, Y. E. (2011). Economic activity and productivity: The role of density in the Greek urban space. European Association of Geographers Annual Meeting "Geography: Your World – A European Perspective", 2–5 June 2011. Athens, Greece.

Doukas, Y. E., Maravegias, N., and Andreou, G. (Eds.). (2022). Η χωρική διάσταση της ευρωπαϊκής ολοκλήρωσης: σύγκλιση ή απόκλιση; Dionicos: Athens, Greece. ISBN: 978-6185-6650-3-6.

Doukas, Y. E., Salvati, L., and Vardopoulos, I. (2023). Unraveling the European Agricultural Policy Sustainable Development Trajectory. Land, 12(9), 1749.

Escolano, J. J., Pedreño, J. N., Lucas, I. G., Almendro Candel, M. B., and Zorpas, A. A. (2018). Decreased Organic Carbon Associated With Land Management in Mediterranean Environments. In M. Á. Muñoz and R. Zornoza (Eds.), Soil Management and Climate Change. Effects on Organic Carbon, Nitrogen Dynamics, and Greenhouse Gas Emissions (pp. 1–13). Elsevier: Cambridge, MA, USA. ISBN: 978-0-12-812128-3

European Environment Agency (2006). Urban Sprawl in Europe. The ignored challenge. European Environment Agency. Copenhagen, DK: Office for Official Publications of the European Communities.

Franci, F., Mandanici, E., and Bitelli, G. (2015). Remote sensing analysis for flood risk management in urban sprawl contexts. Geomatics, Natural Hazards and Risk, 6(5–7), 583–599.

Frenkel, A. and Ashkenazi, M. (2008). Measuring urban sprawl: how can we deal with it? Environment and Planning B: Planning and Design, 35, 56–79.

Frenkel, A., Bendit, E. and Kaplan, S. (2013). The linkage between the lifestyle of knowledge-workers and their intra-metropolitan residential choice: A clustering approach based on self-organizing maps. Computers, Environment and Urban Systems, 39, 151–161

Gallagher, P. (2001). The Environmental, Social, and Cultural Impacts of Sprawl. Natural Resources & Environment, 15(4), 219–267.

Galster, G., Hanson, R., Ratcliffe, M. R., Wolman, H., Coleman, S. and Freihage, J. (2001).Wrestling sprawl to the ground: defining and measuring an elusive concept. Housing Policy Debate, 12(4), 681–717.

Gargiulo Morelli, V. and Salvati, L. (2014). Unveiling Urban Sprawl in the Mediterranean Region: Towards a Latent Urban Transformation? International Journal of Urban and Regional Research, 38(6), 1935–1953.

Glaeser, E. L., and Kahn, M. E. (2004). Sprawl and urban growth. In Handbook of Regional and Urban Economics (pp. 2481–2527). Elsevier.

Hanzl, M. (2010). Urban Sprawl in Europe: Landscapes, Land-use Change and Policy. Planning Practice & Research, 25(2), 273–274.

Hasse, J. E., and Lathrop, R. G. (2003). Land resource impact indicators of urban sprawl. Applied Geography, 23(2–3), 159–175.

Hennig, E. I., Schwick, C., Soukup, T., Orlitová, E., Kienast, F., and Jaeger, J. A. G. (2015). Multi-scale analysis of urban sprawl in Europe: Towards a European de-sprawling strategy. Land Use Policy, 49, 483–498.

Jaeger, J. A. G. and Schwick, C. (2014). Improving the measurement of urban sprawl: Weighted Urban Proliferation (WUP) and its application to Switzerland. Ecological Indicators, 38, 294–308.

Jaeger, J. A. G., Bertiller, R., Schwick, C. and Kienast, F. (2010). Suitability criteria for measures of urban sprawl. Ecological Indicators, 10, 397–406.

Ji, W., Ma, J., Twibell, R. W., and Underhill, K. (2006). Characterizing urban sprawl using multi-stage remote sensing images and landscape metrics. Computers, Environment and Urban Systems, 30(6), 861–879.

Kazepov, Y. (2005). Cities of Europe: Changing Contexts, Local Arrangements, and the Challenge to Urban Cohesion. Oxford: Blackwell.

Keith, M., and Parnell, S. (2023). Risk and Returns: Large-scale Funding for Urban Research. International Journal of Urban and Regional Research, 47(2), 299–304.

Kempton, Y., Salvati, L., and Vardopoulos, I. (2022). Long-term planning and development for urban and regional inclusion, safety, resilience, and sustainability. Insights from Singapore. Region & Periphery, 14(14), 59–79.

King, R., Proudfoot, L. and Smith, B. (1997). The Mediterranean. Environment and society. London: Arnold.

Lemonakis, C., Alexopoulos, G., Garefalakis, A., and Garefalakis, S. (2024). Trends and new elements in urban hierarchy research: the Greek paradigm. The Annals of Regional Science, 72, 335–354.

Lu, J., Li, B., Li, H., and Al-Barakani, A. (2021). Expansion of city scale, traffic modes, traffic congestion, and air pollution. Cities, 108, 102974.

Meles, T. H. H., Farrell, N., and Curtis, J. (2023). How well do building energy performance certificates predict heat loss? Energy Efficiency, 16(7), 1–25.

Montero, E., Van Wolvelaer, J., and Garzón, A. (2014). The European Urban Atlas. In I. Manakos and M. Braun (Eds.), Land Use and Land Cover Mapping in Europe. Remote Sensing and Digital Image Processing (pp. 115–124). Springer.

Musterd, S. and Ostendorf, W. (1998). Urban segregation and the welfare state: Inequality and exclusion in western cities. (London: Routledge).

Orenstein, D. E., Frenkel, A. and Jahshan, F. (2014). Methodology matters: measuring urban spatial development using alternative methods, Environment and Planning B: Planning and Design, 41, 3–23

Patacchini, E., and Zenou, Y. (2009). Urban sprawl in Europe. Brookings-Wharton Papers on Urban Affairs, 125–149.

Pisarevskaya, A., Scholten, P., and Kaşlı, Z. (2022). Classifying the Diversity of Urban Diversities: an Inductive Analysis of European Cities. Journal of International Migration and Integration, 23(2), 655–677.

Rees, W. and Wackernagel, M. (1996). 'Urban ecological footprints: Why cities cannot be sustainable—And why they are a key to sustainability', Environmental Impact Assessment Review, 16(4–6), 223–248.

Ridolfi, E., Pujol, D. S., Ippolito, A., Sarantakou, E., and Salvati, L. (2017). An urban political ecology approach to local development in fast-growing, tourism-specialized coastal cities. Tourismos, 12(1), 171–204.

Rodríguez-Cuenca, B., and Alonso, M. (2014). Semi-Automatic Detection of Swimming Pools from Aerial High-Resolution Images and LIDAR Data. Remote Sensing, 6(4), 2628–2646.

Salvati, L. (2015). Lost in complexity, found in dispersion: 'Peripheral' development and deregulated urban growth in Rome. Cities, 47, 73–80.

Salvati, L., and Carlucci, M. (2015). Land-use structure, urban growth, and periurban landscape: a multivariate classification of the European cities. Environment and Planning B: Planning and Design, 42(5), 801–829.

Salvati, L., and Carlucci, M. (2016). Patterns of Sprawl: The Socioeconomic and Territorial Profile of Dispersed Urban Areas in Italy. Regional Studies, 50(8), 1346–1359.

Salvati, L., Gargiulo Morelli, V., Rontos, K. and Sabbi, A. (2013b). Latent Exurban Development: City Expansion Along the Rural-To-Urban Gradient in Growing and Declining Regions of Southern Europe. Urban Geography, 34(3), 376–394.

Salvati, L., Gitas, I., Di Giacomo, T. V., Sarantakou, E., and Carlucci, M. (2017). Sprawl matters: the evolution of fringe land, natural amenities and disposable income in a Mediterranean urban area. Environment Development and Sustainability, 19, 727–743.

Salvati, L., Munafo, M., Morelli, V. G., and Sabbi, A. (2012). Low-density settlements and land use changes in a Mediterranean urban region. Landscape and Urban Planning, 105(1–2), 43–52.

Salvati, L., Ridolfi, E., Pujol, D. S., and Ruiz, P. S. (2016). Latent sprawl, divided Mediterranean landscapes: urban growth, swimming pools, and the socio-spatial structure of Athens, Greece. Urban Geography, 37(2), 296–312.

Salvati, L., Ridolfi, E., Zambon, I., Serra, P., and Sauri, D. (2015). Swimming Pools as Indicator of Urban Sprawl: an Exploratory Analysis in a Mediterranean City. International Journal of Environmental Research, 9(4), 1325–1332.

Salvati, L., Zambon, I., Chelli, F. M., and Serra, P. (2018). Do spatial patterns of urbanization and land consumption reflect different socioeconomic contexts in Europe? Science of The Total Environment, 625, 722–730.

Salvati, L., Zitti, M., and Sateriano, A. (2013). Changes in city vertical profile as an indicator of sprawl: Evidence from a Mediterranean urban region. Habitat International, 38, 119–125.

Schneider, A. and Woodcock, C. E. (2008). Compact, dispersed, fragmented, extensive? A comparison of urban growth in twenty-five global cities using remotely sensed data, pattern metrics and census information. Urban Studies, 45(3), 659–692.

Serra, P. Vera, A. and Tulla, A. F. (2013). Spatial and Socioenvironmental Dynamics of Catalan Regional Planning from a Multivariate Statistical Analysis Using 1980s and 2000s Data. European Planning Studies, 22(6), 1280–1300.

Shao, Z., Sumari, N. S., Portnov, A., Ujoh, F., Musakwa, W., and Mandela, P. J. (2021). Urban sprawl and its impact on sustainable urban development: a combination of remote sensing and social media data. Geo-Spatial Information Science, 24(2), 241–255.

Smiraglia, D., Salvati, L., Egidi, G., Salvia, R., Giménez-Morera, A., and Halbac-Cotoara-Zamfir, R. (2021). Toward a New Urban Cycle? A Closer Look to Sprawl, Demographic Transitions and the Environment in Europe. Land, 10(2), 127.

Sudhira, H. S., Ramachandra, T. V., and Jagadish, K. S. (2004). Urban sprawl: metrics, dynamics and modelling using GIS. International Journal of Applied Earth Observation and Geoinformation, 5(1), 29–39.

Surya, B., Salim, A., Hernita, H., Suriani, S., Menne, F., and Rasyidi, E. S. (2021). Land Use Change, Urban Agglomeration, and Urban Sprawl: A Sustainable Development Perspective of Makassar City, Indonesia. Land, 10(6), 556.

Theobald, D. M. (2001). Land-Use Dynamics Beyond the American Urban Fringe. Geographical Review, 91(3), 544–564.

Tombolini, I., Rodrigo-Comino, J., and Salvati, L. (2022). Land Quality and Sustainable Urban Forms. Changing Landscapes and Socioeconomic Structures of European Cities. Springer.

Torrens, P. M. (2008). A toolkit for measuring sprawl. Applied Spatial Analysis and Policy, 1, 5–36.

Tsai, Y. H. (2005). Quantifying urban form: compactness versus 'sprawl'. Urban Studies, 42(1), 141–161

Vardopoulos, I. (2019). Environmental impact assessment scoping report. Residential complex in Rafina - Pikermi city, Greece. Sustainable Development, Culture, Traditions Journal, 1(A), 63–79.

Vardopoulos, I. (2023). Adaptive reuse for sustainable development and land use: A multivariate linear regression analysis estimating key determinants of public perceptions. Heritage, 6(2), 809–828.

Vardopoulos, I., Ioannides, S., Georgiou, M., Voukkali, I., Salvati, L., and Doukas, Y. E. (2023). Shaping sustainable cities: A long-rerm GIS-emanated spatial analysis of settlement growth and planning in a coastal Mediterranean European city. Sustainability, 15(14), 11202.

Vardopoulos, I., Stamopoulos, C., Chatzithanasis, G., Michalakelis, C., Giannouli, P., and Pastrapa, E. (2020). Considering urban development paths and processes on account of adaptive reuse projects. Buildings, 10(4), 73.

Vermeiren, K., Crols, T., Uljee, I., De Nocker, L., Beckx, C., Pisman, A., Broekx, S., and Poelmans, L. (2022). Modelling urban sprawl and assessing its costs in the planning process: A case study in Flanders, Belgium. Land Use Policy, 113, 105902.

Vidal, M., Domene, E. and Sauri, D. (2011). Changing geographies of water-related consumption: residential swimming pools in suburban Barcelona. Area, 43(1), 67–75.

Vinci, S., Vardopoulos, I., and Salvati, L. (2023). A tale of a shrinking City? Exploring the complex interplay of socio-demographic dynamics in the recent development of Attica, Greece. Cities, 132, 104089.

Wardrop, N. A., Jochem, W. C., Bird, T. J., Chamberlain, H. R., Clarke, D., Kerr, D., Bengtsson, L., Juran, S., Seaman, V., and Tatem, A. J. (2018). Spatially disaggregated population estimates in the absence of national population and housing census data. Proceedings of the National Academy of Sciences, 115(14), 3529–3537.

Welch, R. (1982). Spatial resolution requirements for urban studies. International Journal of Remote Sensing, 3(2), 139–146.

Zambon, I., and Salvati, L. (2018). Swimming Pools: A Landmark of Sprawl. Mediterranean Urbanity, Landscape Architecture and Social Issues. Nova Science: Hauppauge, NY, USA.

Zambon, I., Sabbi, A., Schuetze, T., and Salvati, L. (2015). Exploring forest 'fringescapes': urban growth, society and swimming pools as a sprawl landmark in coastal Rome. Rendiconti Lincei, 26(2), 159–168.

Zambon, I., Serra, P., Sauri, D., Carlucci, M., and Salvati, L. (2017). Beyond the 'Mediterranean city': socioeconomic disparities and urban sprawl in three Southern European cities. Geografiska Annaler: Series B, Human Geography, 99(3), 319–337.

Index

About the Authors

Ioannis Vardopoulos studied civil engineering and did his postgraduate studies first in environmental management and conservation and later in sustainable development with honors distinction. Holding a doctorate in applied urban sustainability, he conducts high-quality research toward addressing key concerns of the contemporary built environment through principles of applied sustainability and circular economy. His research interests include a wide range of urban and regional sustainability aspects. [www.ivardopoulos.com].

Francisco Escrivà Saneugenio is a geographer, proficient in environmental studies, territorial analysis, and cartography, currently serving the University of Valencia as Associate Lecturer and Researcher at the Department of Geography, while pursuing his doctorate in environmental geography at the Oviedo University. His research focuses on topics including physical, human, and economic geography, climate change, urbanization, housing policies, and sustainable development, particularly in the context of the Mediterranean region. Significant contributions to the academic world include scientific articles published in prestigious scholarly journals, book chapters, and books, meticulously composed to captivate the international audience.

Adele Sateriano is an accomplished lawyer, ministerial official, and independent scholar based in Rome, Italy. Her research delves into the complexities of environmental law, urban planning, and policy implications on land use, as well as demographic shifts and migration patterns. Dr. Sateriano's scholarly output, whether as the (co-)author or editor, has been accepted for publication in highly respected international journals and academic books.

Luca Salvati is an economic geography statistics Senior Researcher and Professor at the Sapienza University of Rome, Italy. A renowned expert in institutional statistics, statistics for the territory, and the theory of indicators, with a focus on regional and urban economics, housing policy, spatial planning, and indication theory. Ranked in the top 2% of the most influential scientists in the world, Dr. Salvati has authored more than 700 scientific publications covering topics on economic statistics, monetary evaluation of natural resources, urban economy, regional demography, and spatial analysis.

For Product Safety Concerns and Information please contact our
EU representative GPSR@taylorandfrancis.com Taylor & Francis
Verlag GmbH, Kaufingerstraße 24, 80331 München, Germany